Sugar in My Grits

GRIEF TO GRATITUDE
THROUGH GRACE

AMANDA Y. CALLENDER

JDELANO PUBLISHING

ISBN (Print): 978-1-73458-920-7
ISBN (eBook): 978-1-73458-921-4

Library of Congress Control Number: 2020903744

Cover Image: Amanda Callender

Published by: JDelano Publishing
P.O. BOX 522
Lincoln Park, NJ 07035
www.jdelanopublishing.com

Printed in the United States of America

To my Son…

Jax Delano Callender,

You are my greatest joy and my biggest fear.

Thank you for being my mirror.

Mommy loves you.

Dr. George Jenkins, DMD, MHA

Foreword

by

Dr. George Jenkins, DMD

I'm not an overly religious person, but there is something power-fully spiritual about what you are about to read. I lost my mom to cancer, two weeks prior when something compelled Kayla (Amanda's wife) to have this manuscript sent to me. "He may need it", she said. Being in my own cloud of grief, I wasn't too sure of anything. I wasn't certain if I would ever be the same husband, friend, mentor or community servant, ever again. Questioning what was happening while sensing my generosity eroding rapidly. It's hard to explain really. It was as if I was slowly being drained of my superpower. And then I opened the mail.

The timing and content felt like it fell out of the sky with postage marks on the package addressed just for me. Amanda sharing her journey has helped me to embark on my very own journey towards emotional victory. Through the sheer force of her personality, experi-ences and perspective Amanda has given the world a tremendous gift with these words. It is at once, an orientation manual and group therapy session, for those who have experienced loss or those attempting to understand a loved one who has. And that is all of us. I would be remiss if I didn't thank Kayla for her persistence. Thank you Kayla. I hope you all enjoy your session with Amanda. I am extremely grateful to her for mine.

Acknowledgements

I would like to thank God for being who he is - Omnipotent. He gets all the praise. I'm nothing without his Grace and Blessings.

To my wife, Mrs. Kayla Callender you make me better. Thank you for waiting. I couldn't be who I am without your love and patience. I love you 25/8.

My amazing friends and family that sent me texts saying, "finish that book". I humbly thank you.

To AK, thank you for helping me find my voice. There is no way I could have completed this book without you.

Traci, over a waterfall in a barrel.

Khairah, thank you will never be enough.

To all my angels, thank you for guiding me.

Mommy, I miss you so much.

Disclaimer

I have tried to recreate events, locales and conversations from my memories of them. In order to maintain their anonymity in some instances I have changed the names of individuals and places, I may have changed some identifying characteristics and details such as physical properties, occupations and places of residence.

INTRODUCTION

There's a decade old debate in the black community about whether sugar belongs in grits. BELONGS?! Who decides that? There seems to be this overwhelming list of, "for the culture" requirements, that sets off unnecessary anxiety in us all. For example, the family first myth or the family over everything belief. Please don't misunderstand me; family is a very important vital part of our development and sense of belonging. However, I believe there is an idiotic sentiment that people shouldn't be held accountable for their actions because we are 'a family.' We must stop inviting the uncle that molested his niece to the cookout; baby girl is dying inside. Seeing him gives her anxiety. "What happens in this house stays in this house," is killing us. You aren't supposed to utilize your life jacket on a sinking ship because the captain is your brother? That's ridiculousness. I'm jumping ship, then warning everyone else he can't sail, and for them to save themselves. There is a fear that if outsiders notice you symbolically jumping ship, it shines a light on the family's imperfections. God forbid we do that. Everyone wants to appear to have it all together. Apparently, appearances are everything to some people.

There is disbelief that we aren't affected by generational curses. We must first acknowledge they exist. Why is there contentment in struggling with the same bondages as our parents? – the notion that vulnerability is a sign of weakness; depression is all in your head and we're supposed to "push through" grief; moreover, you better not admit it if you can't play spades. Oh, the pressure. Amid all this muck and mire, I must worry about someone's judgment if I sprinkle sugar in my grits? Wow!

I've struggled to deal with grief and pain without knowing that mourning is a journey. You can't turn it off and on like a light switch. It's a process that cannot be rushed. Mourning is like wading water; sometimes the water comes up around your neck. Panicking won't help. I've seen people grapple with familial hurt that has festered like an untreated wound, destroying generations, and depriving them of their potential for greatness. Life's a balancing act and sometimes our hands are juggling issue after issue. With no support, we must walk the tight rope of life from one end of the circus tent to the other. All the while, hoping, praying, and having faith that if by chance we fall, God's Grace is more sufficient than the flimsy net set up to catch us. If we fall, because fall we may, where do we get the confidence and support to get back up and try it again?

In order to walk into our purpose, we must acknowledge our grief, work through anxiety and release the pain of the past. Therefore, some things just must come out.

To help

To heal

To reveal

To grow

To live

To inspire.

To sweeten life just a little bit.

Like sugar in my grits.

TABLE OF CONTENTS

Sugar in My Grits

GRIEF TO GRATITUDE
THROUGH GRACE

"He who has a why to live can
bear almost any how."

—Fredrick Nietzsche [1]

Chapter 1

Why

Why is grief so heavy? It sat on my chest like an elephant. It weighed on me like a wet tarp over a damaged roof in the rain. Grief broke my spirit. It stole my smile, introduced me to insomnia, and then had the nerve to interfere with my judgment. I was lost, broken and no longer myself. Heck no! I don't own the patent on grief. I'm not the only one that's ever been sad, but the loneliness that accompanies it makes you think you are. Sure, everyone grieves for someone or something. However, I couldn't help but think or hope that no one has ever felt this much pain. I don't just mean physical pain. I mean emotional agony. The pain of a broken heart. The pain of trying to catch your breath after crying hours on end. It changes you; alters your perception of happiness.

Early on in life, I was taught cause and effect. THIS happened so THAT transpired. Therefore, I have this inherent need to understand the reasons behind events and people's actions. It's just the way that my brain was trained to work. I am always trying to figure out the "why" of everything. Because of my thought process I didn't understand why my therapist could not explain the actions of my cousin's murderer. Nor could she explain the reasons for what I deemed at the time was the selfishness of my parents. You see, I went to her seeking answers. I mean, that's what therapists do, right? Tell us why bad things happen? Help us to figure out why? No? Well that's why I went to see one. I thought if I understood "why", I could deal with the grief. However, the best she could tell me was, "Amanda, there is good and evil in this world and some people are just plain evil. What happened to your cousin was evil; there is no other explanation for that. As far as your parents goes, good people tend to make bad choices that sometimes affects everyone, especially their offspring."

I thought, "Huh?" My mind immediately went to the infamous quote from the popular 80's show, Different Strokes, "What you talking 'bout Willis?" As she stared at me right then, I knew she couldn't cure me. I knew she didn't know "why," and this would be a long journey. I had so much emotional trauma that I didn't know how to describe. I was broken in ways unbeknownst to me, that required more work on my part than hers. But nonetheless here I was thinking she could somehow "cure" me. I was at the end of my rope and I thought she had all the answers. I'm not ashamed to say I lost my mind for a little while. I am a Certified Biomedical Technician – I make things work. However, I couldn't fix myself. I could repair expensive medical equipment, but I couldn't fix the hole in my heart. I didn't know how to make the agony stop. I felt so useless.

After our first session I imagined her taking a drink from a bottle of liquor she had stashed away in her desk drawer. I mean, after all, alcohol helped me, or so I thought. It took me years to even realize I needed therapy. I thought being sad and angry was normal. Let me clarify. Being sad and angry is very normal. However, it's not normal that sad and angry goes to bed with you, to work with you, or to the grocery store. Sad and angry is like a dynamic duo of depression that breaks up relationships and destroys the core of your soul in a single bound. It took years of my bad attitude, broken relationships, and two tragedies to realize I couldn't go on like that. Something had to give, and that something was me. I broke. I literally felt like Humpty Dumpty and I longed to be whole again.

My pain stemmed from the sadness of my grief and in turn made me angry with God. For a long time, I didn't pray, and I found myself not speaking to Him. You know, like a teenager, when a parent says they can't go to the mall with their friends. I stomped off to my room slamming the door behind me, vowing to never speak to the big guy again. I would eventually learn to fake a laugh and smile again, but I was a different person. I masked my grief with anger. For me, it was easier to be angry than sad. Anger didn't require my tears. I think that's why I stayed sad for so long. It was my resentment. Missing my parents made me think of them often uncovering a lot of animosity. It's a daunting task being angry at a dead person. It's hard to expel those feelings.

Here's a little secret. Death doesn't negate anger. Whatever feelings you have for a person doesn't go into the coffin with them. My anger didn't burn with my mother's remains during her cremation. My anger wasn't with my dad in the ground at Rosehill Cemetery. Contrarily, the feelings lingered on like the smell of burnt popcorn in the microwave inside a room with no windows. Well, at least that's how it was for me. My parents' death was hard, but I didn't show it at the time. Why was it so hard for me to express my hurt?

I pushed my way through the deaths of my grandmothers. Yes, maternal and paternal. However, my cousin's murder broke me. Not in half but into tiny little pieces. By the time my nephew tragically died, I was just numb. Ready to be fit for a strait jacket. I imagined myself in one of those rubber rooms I had seen on TV, drooling from the mouth. I retreated to the solitude of my mind, not caring how difficult it would be to get out.

Grief was more than emotional suffering for me. It led to depression, which started to take toll on my body. I noticed some of my physical characteristics changed as well. I had a slump in my posture, and I started to walk slower. Grief and depression tend to co-mingle because of similar traits, but they are different. Some people are born with the chemical imbalance that causes depression. Other people just have their hearts ripped out and then have trouble coping. I think I fall somewhere in the middle ground - if there even is one. People tend to manage grief better than depression; or, so they think. I thought I was managing my parents' death, not knowing it was affecting my behavior in my relationship. I was angry, short tempered, and could go long periods of time by myself. I felt as if death was relentless towards me. I would drift off into a daze and wonder, why me? As soon as I thought I was improving, someone else died.

If I averaged it out, some of the closest people to me died within 18 months of each other for 11 years straight. Let me rephrase that. Over the course of 11 years, every year and a half, someone close to me died. Got it now? Can you imagine that? Neither could I, but nevertheless it's my story.

"Never complain about what your parents
couldn't give you, it was probably all they had."

—Unknown

CHAPTER 2

Meet The Parents

Both of my parents died in 1999. My mother passed away in February, a week before my 25th birthday, and my father passed away in December, two weeks before Christmas. Boy that was some year! Everyone was freaked out about Y2K. Another big thing that never happened. The initial impact of my parents' death on me wasn't evident until some years later. I buried the pain deep inside to keep from dealing with the feelings. I was never good at expressing my emotions, especially vulnerability. I cannot be sure if this was an inherited trait from my parents or a defense mechanism I acquired growing up in the inner city. Let me back it up a little bit. I wasn't raised by my parents my entire life. My parents were never married, and they separated around the time I was three years old. I was primarily raised by my maternal grandmother because of my mother's intermittent drug use. The norm for some kids was to be being surprised if someone was on drugs, especially your parents. Not where I am from. My normal was being surprised if they weren't on drugs. Drug abuse and was all around me.

We grew up in the Stella Wright Housing Projects on Prince Street in the Central Ward of Newark, New Jersey. The Central Ward was the heart of Newark. My mother had four kids. She had three girls and one boy. Steffi, Tiffany, myself and Lacy Jr. We were 3 years apart in age and had a very close relationship. We all had different dads, so each of us had siblings on our paternal sides of the family. We never used the words "step" or "half" to describe our other siblings. There was always love from our extended family. I'm pretty sure some people that grew up with us never knew until reading that line. It wasn't a secret we just didn't treat anyone better or less than. We were raised with so much love in that aspect. Like most housing projects, there was high-level unemployment and drug dealing in and around the neighborhood, therefore it wasn't uncommon for the residents to become addicts. Not to mention the 70's and 80's when there was a lot of drug use going on in the inner cities. I grew up in the height of the crack epidemic that ravaged so many families.

My mom as a functioning addict. She may have gotten high, but she worked off and on. She took care of us whenever she could, and when she couldn't, my maternal grandmother lived nearby and would assist. Two blocks away from the projects, believe it or not, were nice garden apartments with benches that weren't missing the slats, manicured lawns, and playgrounds that didn't have broken bottles strewn about. It was High Park Gardens. It was a stark contrast from the projects. By the time I was around eight years old, we were staying there with my grandmother full time. We made new friends in the neighborhood, yet we were still close enough to keep in touch with our old friends and not switch schools.

Sometimes, there were long periods when I didn't see my mother. The inconsistency worried me; thinking back this could have been what would set off the beginning stages of anxiety. No child should have to worry about their parents. I always thought something bad happened during the longer periods of her not being around. I never asked where she had been, I was just happy to see her. Then there were times when she came to stay with us for a month or two. Those times were the best and I remember her being there whenever I got home from school.

I would rush home and drop my book bag in the middle of the living room floor and run to the kitchen where I knew she was. I would sit at the kitchen table as she cooked dinner and babbled on and on about my day. I would randomly stare at her and smile. When she smiled back, I would scan her face taking note of every feature – her perfect eyebrows, big smile, and high cheekbones. I was trying to remember every detail. I followed her around the house, because just maybe she wouldn't be there tomorrow. One would think I would have learned to cook by watching her so much, however, watching her to learn wasn't on my agenda. I was watching her to study her personality, to soak up everything about her, and to store in my memory for the days I would miss her. I missed her often.

My mom was brown skinned, short and thin. She wore her hair cut low and always wore huge hoop earrings. Alberta was her name, however everyone call her Lainey. Short for her middle name, Elaine. My grandmother named her after her sister. She loved to read and had the most beautiful handwriting.

By the time I was fifteen, it seems like we were the same height. She loved to watch soap operas and murder mysteries. Murder She Wrote and Columbo were her favorites. Whatever she watched, I watched because I just wanted to be near her. I memorized her scent and mannerisms. I thought she was so hip by the way she spoke – always sarcastic and to the point.

On school nights, we had dinner, baths, and our homework completed by 8:30pm. The nights I dreaded most were hair braiding nights. I was so tender headed. After my hair was braided, my scalp would burn, and it would feel like little flames were leaping off my head. I would secretly sprinkle water in the parts between the braids in hopes of distinguishing the imaginary fire. She didn't care. Her only concern was making sure we were properly groomed and neat. She would do all three of our heads in one night. I always volunteered to go last, in hopes she would be too tired to finish. Her fatigue didn't make it any easier on my scalp. This is the primary reason for me wearing locs in my hair today. No one has put their hands in my hair for the last 20 years; tender headed is an understatement.

All my friends thought my mom was so cool because she allowed us to talk about anything with her. There was nothing I was afraid to ask my mom for or talk to her about. Her motto was, "If you are honest with me about it, you won't have to sneak and do it." Let's not confuse this with her giving us everything we wanted. No way, not the case. There is big difference in having everything you need verses everything you want. We were just allowed the freedom of discussion.

School was always a priority, but I never felt pressured or stressed about my grades or extracurricular activities. She always asked if I did my best. If I said yes, she would say, "Then that's all I can ask for." Ma, as I affectionately called her when I wanted something, was an only child. Her girlfriends were more like my aunts. She would have friends over, and they would listen to music, drink, talk, dance, and just have a good time. I would always conveniently have to use to bathroom, in order to leave my room, just to get a glimpse of all the action and watch them dance. Boy, my mom could dance. If I inherited anything from her, it wasn't that. When her friends didn't come over, she would head out with them to the local bar. Their favorite was Bill's on the corner of West Kinney Street and Belmont Avenue. I would peek inside while waiting for my grandmother to pick us up. She would put so many quarters in the juke box and dance for hours; all alone; in her own little world. This went on for as long as I can remember.

Just as I was graduating high school in 1992, my mom found out she had contracted HIV. I can't remember how she broke the news to us. Matter of fact, I think she let my grandmother tell us. I don't know if she was ashamed, but I do know she was afraid. Not so much of dying, because of her faith and the many advances happening in the medical community surrounding people being able to live longer with the virus. I felt like she was afraid of not being able to live life on her terms anymore – free. Living with HIV required a regime of medicine and doctor's visits that she wasn't used to. Drug use is already hard on the body, couple that with the HIV virus, and one is bound to shorten their lifespan.

I assumed she would stop the drug use and try to live longer. She didn't. She continued her lifestyle on her terms. Over the years, she deteriorated in health, so she moved back in with my grandmother. She was around a lot more. I guess the sickness slowed her down a bit but didn't stop the drug use completely. Even though I had moved out I was at my grandmother's often. My mom was in and out of the hospitals and rehab facilities and it was taking a toll on my grandmother. My mother was my grandma's only child and she tried to take care of my mom, no matter how old she was or how sickly she was herself. It's a parental instinct; you either have it or not.

My grandmother couldn't get around as good as she used to, so I would check on my mom for her. Between hospitals and rehab facilities, I felt like I was a parent myself. Some days I felt proud when mom would tell hospital staff, "That's my baby girl." Other days I was angry about her absence in my life and her unwillingness to fight the disease, so I didn't want to see her. My emotions were all over the place. Just as I was getting used to her consistently being around, suddenly she was gone. Well, it seemed sudden to me. I felt like we were getting to know each other, until death reached out and called her number.

That's how death is – HERE then GONE. When she died, I didn't know how to process the hurt, so I swallowed it. I literally took a big gulp to hold back whatever emotions I had. I didn't say anything for five days; I got up, took a deep breath, a big gulp, and went on about my life. I had to look in the mirror and say my name, just to make sure I still had a voice. You know, after you have had a tooth extracted and the Novocain wears off, you do this silly looking mouth movements in the mirror. I should have known then that I was losing my mind. I remember going back to work a week later and my boss looked at me and said, "I didn't expect to see you so soon." What's considered "soon" when your mother dies? Just so we are clear, there is no amount of days you can take off to recover from losing your mother. I didn't even tell all my friends.

Back in 1999 when three-way calling was popular, I remember a group of my friends calling to say happy birthday. When I didn't respond with the expected amount of excitement, they inquired what was wrong. I simply said, "My mom died," and continued the conversation. "Mandy!" they shrieked in unison. "Why didn't you tell us?" I'm not sure if I was trying to pretend it didn't happen or what. I only knew the pain kept me paralyzed and I didn't like not being in control of my feelings. It made me feel weak. It made me vulnerable and I didn't want to feel that. Later, I realized it was my anger. I was mad at her for dying, so I didn't think she deserved my tears and emotions. There were mother-daughter moments that I was going to miss tremendously. Not to mention memories we would never get to create. She would never get to be a grandmother to my kids.

Some days when she promised she would come back and she never came, I would be so disappointed and sad. However, in my mind the time we spent together in the end, kind of made up for that lost time. My feelings were all over the place. Maybe I was a depressed kid; I don't know. For the most part, I can remember happiness and having a good childhood. Then there are times I can remember sadness and missing her. Growing up I kept these feelings to myself because I felt like my grandmother was dealing with enough raising us. Because of this, I didn't say much, but I read a lot. I escaped into stories as a kid. I loved to read. I got amazing grades and always listened to my elders. I thought if I was a "good kid" my mom would stay clean more often or for good. Kids tend to think their parents' behavior is their fault; I was one of them.

I shuffled through the months after her death trying to keep a bit of normalcy, whatever that was. I was trying not to miss her, but I did. I missed her tremendously. I was doing everything in my power not to slow down. I picked up extra hours at work and kept my face in a book. I even started spending more time with my dad, thinking it would make things better, but it didn't. Not to mention, he was sick as well. Knowing my dramatic self, I'm pretty sure I fell to the ground at some point kicking and screaming. In my mind I had all sorts of tantrums. I thought God was surely punishing me for something I had done but couldn't remember. I never imagined my mother dying that early in my life. Especially, not before she got her life together.

I think I was holding out hope for that more than anything. Nothing hurts more than your cherished desires not only never coming to fruition, but to come crashing down around you. That's what her death felt like. An avalanche of pain and hope that would never be fulfilled. Thinking back to the days before my mother died, my grandmother advised me to go check on her in the hospital. She had been there for a couple of weeks not doing too well. I remember yelling back at her, "What about the times she didn't check on me? What about the times I needed her?" That's when I realized I was so hurt and angry. I would later regret my stubbornness, of course.

On the evening of February 19,1999, my pager went off several times, but I ignored it (- they were popular back then). I was having a relaxing evening at home with my friend Toni. We were just hanging out and watching movies. Each time she advised me to answer it; each time I declined. A couple of hours and missed pages later, it was apparent that we had fallen asleep, when we were awoken by the ring of the doorbell. It had to have been about 1am. "These folks must have the wrong door," I thought, as I sleepily walked to the steps; they simply would not stop ringing it. I was angry. One of the worse things a person can do is interrupt my slumber. I was the only tenant that lived in the 3-family unit, so these unwanted and ill timely guests had to be for me or Toni. As I opened the door to the apartment, I kneeled slightly to see if I could get a peek at the front door on the lower level in order to see who the culprit was. As I bent down, I could see my oldest sister Steffi, peering through the window. Our eyes met instantly and then I saw her tears. I collapsed at the top step and let out the shrillest scream ever.

Toni heard me and rushed to me from inside the apartment. My eyes never left from Steffi's face. I knew why she was there. Not to mention, I could see our dad, Lacy Sr behind her. This wasn't a social call. I was stuck at the top step. Not one of my limbs would move. This had never happened to me before. Toni had to rush past me, down the steps to open the door for Steffi and our dad. Once she opened the door, I just stared at her, shaking my head back and forth. I knew why they were there at that point. Our mom was gone.

My sister and dad consoled me for what seemed like hours right there on that top step. I cried so hard. All I could think was I didn't check on her. I should have checked on her. I hadn't seen her in days. She had been in the hospital, but I figured I would get around to it. Then I realized that guilt was trying to edge out my grief. We talked a lot. She knew she was going to die. If nothing else, she believed in God and wasn't afraid to physically leave this earth. My mom had one request of me during our conversations in her sickness. She said, "Mandy, I was an only child growing up and I was lonely at times. Please just don't let me die alone." What did I do? In my anger, I let her die alone. I didn't get a chance to say goodbye. I think I wanted one of those Hollywood soap opera goodbyes. You know the one. The one where the person is on their deathbed, and before taking their last breath, manages to impart some wisdom, disclose a family secret, or issue a long-awaited apology. I got no such thing. I was angry she didn't try and save herself. My mother knew she had HIV for years and didn't change her lifestyle. I thought she loved the drugs more than me.

I wanted her to know how it felt to want and need me, and then not show up. The possibility that she could die before such a realization, never crossed my mind. Maybe because I was so angry.

On February 19, 1999, Alberta Elaine Preston died of complications from AIDS. I read the death certificate for years trying to get a sense of closure. Why didn't she stop using drugs once she knew? One of the biggest hurdles in life is forgiveness… of oneself. The hardest thing for me to do, would be to forgive myself for not going to see her when my grandmother told me to.

I still wondered if she forgave herself for the life she lived. Maybe she loved her life, and I was the one who wished things were different.

Back then, I didn't know that alcoholism and drug addiction were diseases. I correlated addicts not stopping the abuse of drugs, to them not loving their family or themselves enough to do so – selfishness. How can someone knowingly continue a behavior that has deathly consequences? Not to mention, leave behind people that love you... PEOPLE YOU LOVE in the process – selfishness. I just didn't understand, and my anger didn't allow me to even begin to try to.

My father, Irving Callender was a very handsome man. He had these grey eyes that seemed to pierce through your soul whenever he looked your way. It was as if he was looking through you and not at you. He had fair skin, thick black hair, and a stocky build. His smile was more like a smirk. Like he knew something that you didn't or was content with keeping a secret in his head all to himself. My dad was very athletic in high school, running track and playing football. He was a ladies' man from what I heard. In his high school yearbook, his favorite pastime is listed as "GIRLS". He was the oldest of my nana's seven kids, and his grandmother nicknamed him the Duke of Callender. He and my mom had me in their early twenties. A couple of years later, he had a son with another woman. My brother was the spitting image of my dad. I'm going to assume my mom forgave him and they stayed together a little while after my brother was born, because I remember him coming over to our house as a kid.

My mom would always say, "Kids aren't responsible for their parent's behavior." Irv, as my dad was affectionately called, also served this country in the Vietnam War. Not just any branch, he was a Marine. That slogan always stuck in my head – "The Few, The Proud, The Marines." Like many other soldiers, he came home with a bunch of nightmares and a drug habit. I was too young to remember, but my mom would tell me stories about how he would hide under the bed or wake up rambling in cold sweats. Even when I got older, he never said much about Vietnam. Only that it was "bad" over there and how he had to kill a kid or be killed by a kid. I'm not sure what that would do to my psyche either. I can't imagine having to go through such a thing and then live with all the horrible memories.

Since my parents didn't stay together long, I don't remember much about my dad as a young kid. I do remember him being at my nana's (his mother) house some weekends when I went over. He brought the occasional birthday and Christmas gift. After dating a nice woman for many years, they eventually got married. My brother and I were in the wedding along with her two children. I still have the VHS tape of the entire event. I remember my family being so happy. Unfortunately, the marriage didn't last long; I can't say why for sure.

I do know that my dad struggled with alcohol and drugs. Just like my mom, he kept a job through it all, until he couldn't anymore. Once his only sister passed away, the drugs and alcohol abuse got worse. His marriage failed, and he moved back in with Nana. People rarely admit they are having trouble coping. Most take up toxic behaviors that give them the illusion of dealing with their issues. During my early twenties, my dad's stocky build diminished, and he had trouble walking. I visited Nana more to be around him, if nothing else but to be close and get to know him. Unfortunately, that only lasted a couple of years. Unlike my mom, I was there when my father died. I was literally in the room. He had a bad infection in his arm from drug use that turned into sepsis. Yes, both my parents were drug addicts. It took me a long time to be able to say that; nevertheless, be transparent and vulnerable enough to write it. I'm not here to pretend; healing requires honesty.

I remember getting a call at work from his doctor, saying they wanted to do an emergency surgery to remove his arm and save his life. My dad and his wife had been estranged for years and I was the oldest child. I had just gotten a promotion at work that came with a huge office. Who knew the first decision I would have to make at my fancy desk would be whether to let a doctor cut my dad's arm off?

Irving Callender was an athlete and a former Marine. My brother had just had his namesake. He was a proud grandfather! What would he do if he couldn't play catch with his grandson?! I didn't have time to ponder. "Save his life," I said to the doctor with my head on the desk as the phone's receiver rested on my ear. "Oh, and I'm on my way." I really didn't leave right away. I sat there and stared out the window at the cars in the parking lot, anything to take my mind off what was happening. I worked in Secaucus, New Jersey, and he was in the VA Hospital in Orange, New Jersey.

If you are familiar with New Jersey, you know that's a ride that allows time for some thinking. I was preparing myself for what was next – therapy, rehabilitation; I was sure it would be a lot. They performed surgery for several hours to remove his arm at the site of the infection, but it didn't work. I remember the doctor coming out with his head hung low. I'm not sure if they teach surgeons poker faces in school or not, but this doctor sucked at it. I knew right away something was wrong. The sepsis had spread throughout his body. His organs weren't functioning properly, and his body had started to swell. He was in bad shape and he was put on a ventilator. I left there feeling so defeated. Over the next couple of days, I remember the doctor calling us up to the hospital saying, "It's time to let him go." There was nothing else they could do for him. He wasn't even breathing on his own. My nana called my Uncle Jerry that lived in Florida. Whenever he was summoned to New Jersey aside from her annual birthday party, it was either weddings or funerals. This one was bad news. Once Uncle Jerry got settled, we took my nana and went up to the hospital. My brother declined to go. I couldn't blame him.

The hospital staff let me have a moment alone with my dad before the machines were unplugged. I just stared at him. AGAIN, here I was so hurt and angry, except something was different with my dad. As I stared at him. I realized I didn't have many memories with him like my mom. My eyebrows furrowed as I tried to think harder and summon a memory. A single tear came to my eye as an indication of defeat. All he ever gave me was his face and his name. Sure, he did his part in taking care of me financially, but no memorable daddy-daughter moments popped into my mind. Well, we shared a dance at his wedding, and I can remember briefly resting my head on his chest. He smelled so good. Another memory was a quiet evening at my nana's house (which was very rare); he and I watched Dances with Wolves. I will always remember how his beard felt against my cheeks whenever he leaned down to give me a hug or a kiss.

So, after 25 years, I had only two special memories. That was it. We were out of time. That's how life works though. You look up and the years have moved on without you. Time doesn't wait until we get our act together. Again, I was stuck. This time, it was at the foot of his hospital bed, just staring at him. The doctor came back in and informed me it was time. I thought that by being at his bedside it would make me feel better about not being at my mom's. It didn't change a thing. I leaned over and kissed his cheek and rubbed his hair. I still wonder if he knew I was there. If he did know I was there and he could speak, what would we possibly say to each other?

The staff moved past me in my daze and began to remove the ventilator, his IV, and the various tubes coming from his body. My focus shifted back and forth from his chest to the vital signs monitor. My body wouldn't move, but my eyes bounced back and forth. The beeping noise that was his heart rate, kept me in a trance for at least 15 minutes.

That's how long it took him to stop breathing once the ventilator was unplugged. Once his chest slowly stopped moving, I thought, "Wow! The two people who made me are gone." I grabbed his hand knowing it would be the last time I would feel him warm. I placed it on my cheek to feel the softness of his fingers against my face. I joked with him once about how soft his hands were. "You can't possibly work hard with hands that soft," I laughed. He fired back with a witty, "I can work hard with a pen you know." I could not believe that the next time I would see him would be in a casket in a room full of sobbing people.

I wouldn't stare into those grey eyes anymore. If you knew my dad, you knew he had the most beautiful eyes. I didn't realize how long I had been standing there until my uncle touched my shoulder and said, "Come my love we have to go tell your brother." My nana, Uncle Jerry, and I held hands and walked in silence to the elevator. I just stared at the floor of the changing tiles as we walked down the quiet ICU hallways. I pushed the elevator button, and as I waited, I looked over at my nana and she said, "I'm so sorry that both your parents are gone now baby." I got the feeling she was trying to save my dad for me. However, I'm not sure I wanted him if he didn't want to do better. Who wants that type of life? I sure as heck didn't.

Talk about a long drive back to the house. We pulled up to my nana's house and just sat there. The house was full of our family knowing what we went to do but awaiting confirmation he was gone. I felt a wave of emotion come over me that I hadn't felt in the hospital. Pulling up to the house made me realize that whenever I came here, my dad wouldn't be here. I got out of the car, walked in the house passed everyone sitting in the living room, ran up the steps, fell out on the bed in his room and cried my eyes out.

On December 13, 1999 Irving Samuel Callender died of sepsis. I hadn't worn a dress since my Prom in the Spring of 1992 and can't remember a time before that. Although I vowed to myself that I wouldn't let clothes define my sexuality, I felt so much more comfortable in pants than a dress and heels. Men's clothes gave me so much more confidence than women's clothes. So, imagine my dismay when Nana came to me a couple of days before my dad's funeral services requesting I wear a dress. I didn't wear a dress to my mother's funeral, why would she ask me to wear one to his? It didn't matter, I just knew I couldn't say no to Nana. The day of the funeral Nana called me into the kitchen. We were all waiting for the family's limo to arrive and take us to the church. She explained that since my dad was a veteran, the Marines would be on hand to give me a flag at the cemetery once the service was over.

I was the oldest child and his wife was not present, so they would present me with the flag. Great, I thought. I get to have a symbol of his service to the country; something to show for all his nightmares he had about the war that my mom told me about. However, before it could sink in Nana said, "Please give the flag to your brother." It was then I knew she was trying to save my dad for my brother. Reluctantly, I agreed just as I had agreed to wear the stupid dress.

My father had a traditional Catholic funeral. Afterwards, we are at the gravesite and I'm sitting in the front row with my legs awkwardly crossed at the ankles because honestly, I didn't know how to sit in a dress. As the Marines so rhythmically folded the flag from dad's coffin, I begin to fidget a bit. After they made this perfect triangle, one of them turns to me, takes two steps, gets down on one knee and looks me directly in my eyes. He said, "Ma'am, on behalf of the President of the United States, the United States Marine Corps, and a grateful nation, please accept this flag as a symbol of our appreciation for your loved one's honorable and faithful service." I think I cried more in that moment than I did during the entire funeral. I'm sure I was crying because Nana asked me to give up the flag and I didn't want to. I stood up and wobbled to my brother as my heels were caught in the dirt beneath my feet. I hugged him while handing him the flag, sobbing all over his suit. I returned to my seat and sat there in my Lane Bryant dress and kitten heels feeling more homely than Moms Mabley.

Looking back, forgiving my father was easier than forgiving my mom. I blamed his drug use on the Vietnam War. Doing this put a reason behind his struggles or should I say an excuse; there is a difference, you know. I gave it a face so to say. Something I could as people say, "put my finger on." I didn't see him much, so we didn't talk often, but he was always around; accessible. I did routinely wonder why some parents don't take more initiative to be involved in the daily lives of their children if they don't live in the house with them.

My brother and I had different childhoods as far as my dad's presence. He lived with our dad at nana's house until my dad moved out. From my understanding visiting my dad at his home weekends as well. He was not the same guy to me as he was to him. I do not need to make up some fairytale myth about who he was. As I began writing this, I thought some hurt and anger would reveal itself as it did regarding my mom. However, the truth is I didn't know my father Irving very well at all. I realized anything that I remember outside of my few memories are stories other people told me that I have kept archived in my brain. It's hard to miss something you never had. I'm sure he was an amazing man.

"Amore a Prima Vista"[2]

Chapter 3

Her

I remember the first time I saw my wife Kayla. It was about a month after my dad's funeral and I was invited to a friend's house party. I was standing off alone in my thoughts, and she seemed to appear out of nowhere. The room got quiet, and everything felt like it was moving in slow motion. I followed her around the room with my eyes, imagining her rocking our baby to sleep. I never believed in love at first sight, until her. I'm not sure if she noticed me standing in the corner alone, with my head down, but I noticed her. My mouth hung open and I couldn't take my eyes off her. I didn't know her name, where she was from, or if she had come to the party with someone else. I didn't care. I just knew that was Mrs. Callender.

I always knew I wanted to get married but seeing her in that moment confirmed it; once I stopped dating men and knew for sure it would be a woman, I couldn't wait to fall in love. Before then, my friends and I used to sit around and talk about HER qualities and our expectations from marriage. We referred to our ideal woman as "HER." We were like the teenage boys from the movie Weird Science with our delusions of grandeur about a perfect mate. It undoubtedly gave us a skewed view of women, expecting them to look and act perfectly. We held them to these impossible standards that we ourselves weren't ready or even capable of upholding.

As the night progressed, we spoke in passing and were involved in a couple of group conversations. I came to find out that Kayla was in a relationship; but I didn't really care. I concocted in my mind that due to losing my parents and my sadness, I deserved whatever I wanted. Later in the evening, I asked the Hostess Dee about Kayla. Before I could get my full thought out, Dee was shaking her head back and forth gesturing no.

"What do you mean no?" I snapped back.

"She's dating someone and you… I just don't think you're ready," Dee said.

"Forget ready! That's my wife," I said.

"No Amanda," was the last thing Dee said to me that evening. I didn't care. I wanted her, so I pursued her. She didn't give in right away; but trust me I was laying it on thick. Not to mention that adage about how you get them is how you lost them, played in my head briefly. However, like I said, I didn't care, and I didn't plan on losing her. I was newly single, yet ready to settle down. It took months but I managed to get a date. After hours of conversation, she confirmed that she was only going out with me because her current relationship was on the rocks; things weren't going well. I saw the door crack open and stuck my foot in it. "This is it Amanda; don't you mess this up," I would tell myself.

For some reason, I thought being a gay single woman would be easier than being a straight single woman. There is no difference. It all equates to loneliness, when you're searching for someone to share life with. I don't think our souls comprehend "sexuality."

Souls comprehend love, compatibility, and trust. A connection that can't be explained, that's what I was longing for. It had nothing to do with sex. I just so happened to have found it in a woman. After getting my heart broken by my first love, it was like my heart and body wouldn't allow me to love another man. Sex was easy, but I couldn't connect to another man after him. I was bisexual for years before I was finally comfortable in my skin. There was an awkward stage where I wasn't quite sure how to dress, walk or talk. I hid my insecurities very well. After some years and a lot of reassurance from my family and friends, I was comfortable in my sexuality. Some people never gain that confidence or support from their family and friends. I'm not sure what the catalyst was for me, but I knew that how I look, dressed, and whom I love should not affect my contributions to society. Who I share my bed with, doesn't affect my ability to do my job. I never spoke about my sexuality because I didn't think it mattered; and I rarely do, to this day. Being gay does not define me. Being a loving human being does. I honestly think labels put us in a box. Once something is labeled, it gives people an idea or expectation of how you're supposed to behave.

As I grew to know love, I realized "love at first sight" is a cute concept, but there is usually a moment when a person decides they want to spend the rest of their life with someone. Once the butterflies are gone and the queasiness has subsided, clarity takes over. For me, it was while Kayla and I were dating. My grandmother had a stroke after my mom passed away and was wheelchair bound. I moved back in with her to help to care for her. Kayla slept over one night and stayed with my grandmother while I went off to work. When I came home, my grandmother had on a change of clothes, dinner was done, and the house was clean. This woman, whom I had known for a couple of months, had taken my ailing grandma from her hospital bed, washed her, dressed her, cooked and fed her. I remember saying to myself, "See, I told you she was the one."

Kayla also gave me room to grow. Relationships should be growing constantly. Once something doesn't have room to grow, it dies; like a plant that outgrows its pot. If you don't move it to a bigger pot to allow the roots to grow, the leaves will begin to wilt and die. Kayla provided me with a bigger pot, sprinkled with patience and an abundance of indescribable unconditional love. She was the sugar in my grits. The sweetness I was looking for. She met my family, and everyone loved her immediately. This was something I had never experienced, especially with my sisters. They were my protectors. As a matter of fact, they still are. Whenever they introduce me, they say, "This is my baby sister." It makes me smile every time. Kayla and I dated for six months, had a world wind romance, and then we decided to move in together. I'm sure some of our friends thought we were crazy, but I was very happy. The year was 2000 and it seemed like it flew by. During that year, we visited her mom in Virginia a couple of times; I loved it. After a year we decided not to renew our lease in New Jersey and move to Virginia Beach.

In August 2001, we quit our jobs, got our security deposit back in cash, packed our furniture up on a one-way haul, and headed down the Eastern Shore. By now, my grandmother was in a nursing home because my siblings and I could no longer take care of her. My sister Steffi worked at the nursing home, so I was comfortable leaving. In Virginia I felt like I was on vacation. The weather was always good, and I fell in love with the ocean immediately.

Six months later, I proposed to Kayla. We were engaged for two years, with Kayla planning most of the ceremony herself. She was always sure of what she wanted. We had a New Year's Eve, evening wedding. I just graduated college and started a new job that day. A few of our family and friends came to town so it was my responsibility to get them settled in, amongst other things. I ended up being two hours late to the ceremony. For some reason I wasn't rushing or stressed about it. I took it all as a sign. Finally, while on my way to the ceremony location I said to myself, "If she's gone, she is not my wife." December 31, 2003, although not legal yet, we had a commitment ceremony with some of our family and close friends. Kayla legally changed her last name to Callender. She waited.

We spent ten years in Virginia Beach, and boy was it a learning experience. Good times, bad times, great times, and financially difficult times. Virginia holds a special place in my heart. I'm not sure I would have made it through my depression without being in her arms. She helped me grow while shielding me from familiar faces and what I perceived as would be judgement from my inability to cope. I went back to school and got my degree there. It became my little slice of heaven that I could retreat to in order to recharge and escape the world. Even today.

Initially, we didn't have any friends there, only a few of Kayla's family members. Basically, we were all we had, so we had to depend on each other more than ever. Love is fragile even when it's strong. It's agreeing to catch someone falling out the sky with their flaws in tow. I never had a doubt she would catch me. She allowed me to dream and she believed in each one of them, no matter how farfetched they seemed. This laid the foundation for the relationship we have today. Trust and honesty being the strongest component.

Years later, my friends Tee and Trina would say, "I can't believe you of all people found HER." Yes, yes, I did. I found HER.

"Blessed are they that mourn: for
they shall be comforted."

(King James Version, Matthew 5.14)

CHAPTER 4

Grief

No matter how much you think you are prepared for the death of a loved one, you never are. You find yourself planting your feet firmly in your best defensive stance and positioning your arms ready to tackle death at any moment. None of that preparation will matter. Death still comes and knocks the wind out of you. Expected or unexpected, it takes your breath away before it snatches your feet from beneath you. Bam! Before you know what hit you, you're flat on your back staring at the sky in pain. Death doesn't play fair. The cards are stacked against you. The best thing you can do is try and brace for impact.

Death can be dark and scary, like your worst nightmare. It sneaks up on you in the middle of the night, snatching the life out of your body. Other times, it's clear and evident, like a church bell on Sunday when service is over, or like a guaranteed death sentence from an incurable disease. Death is definitive. It doesn't matter your religious beliefs or who or what you pray to. No one physically comes back from it so you will have to grieve for them. You will feel grief's emptiness take over your limbs and carry you off to a dark place and strip you of your smile and every other happy emotion you thought you had. You will cry. A LOT! You will not be able to eat. You will not be able to sleep.

Oftentimes, there are no encouraging words to lift your fallen spirits. The days run into the nights, and it feels like sun never shines; or better yet, like it's shining for everyone except you. It's lonely. You think no one understands your pain, so you isolate yourself. It's heavy. You struggle to put one foot in front of the other, that's IF you manage to get out of the bed. It's painful. Most days everything hurts. It's so hard. You may wish you were dead yourself. There is this constant overwhelming sadness in the air. This is grief.

Nana

My nana (paternal grandmother) was cute, cuddly and very lovable. No matter what you did, or said, or how much you messed up, she still loved you. I always thought this was the epitome of unconditional love. Growing up, she lived close by in another housing project named Hayes Homes. As a kid, I visited mostly on weekends. I got to hang out with my cousins and my brother. We went to the movies, or just played outside. I was always welcomed with a great meal and an abundance of hugs. Most of my uncles, cousins and my brother lived in the same house. It felt like we were having one big sleepover. Every Sunday dinner felt like Thanksgiving, with all the people and comradery. It wasn't uncommon in the 70's and 80's to have multiple generations living under the same roof. I didn't see this in my maternal grandmother's house because my mother was an only child. Things were vastly different in the two households.

The older I got the more I visited, because I was able to go on my own. Fast forward to my early twenties, around 1996, I remember sitting in Nana's kitchen eating as usual. It was just me and Nana, which was very rare. She came and sat next to me, squeezed my hand and said, "I know you like girls." It was very random and matter of fact. I dropped my fork which was something I never did and kind of just stared at her. My first instinct was to lie, maybe because I hadn't figured out my sexuality myself; but here was Nana low key outing me. Well, it was just us, but I still felt very vulnerable. Again, vulnerability wasn't my thing.

Before I could lie, she squeezed my hand tighter and reassured me that she loved me no matter what. I hugged her so tightly and quietly cried on her shoulder. She lifted my head and looked down at me over her glasses and smiled and said, "Don't worry; you are going to be okay." It felt like a heavy weight was lifted off my shoulders. She wasn't mad or disappointed or had some long drawn out speech. I hugged her so tightly. Those were the only words that were ever spoken about my sexuality in my family. There was no big coming out party or a younger sibling outing me at the Thanksgiving dinner table giving grandpa a heart attack like we see in the movies. I was so relieved after that encounter. Forget all the boyfriends I had, if you were a woman in my life and met my nana you were special.

As my cousins, my brother and I got older everyone had branched off into their own little world most of them moving out of Nana's house. However, we always made it a point to meet at Nana's on Fridays after work for fish, drinks, and to catch up on what each other had going on. Just like growing up on Sunday's there was always a meal cooked and plenty of laugher. By this time, we were well into our careers and had our own families but made time to sit on the porch and laugh.

We always had jokes about which one of us was consistent or not in our dating lives. Kayla met Nana, my brother and my cousins and they all knew how much I loved her.

One Sunday after dinner Nana and Kayla sat on the porch smoking a forbidden cigarette. They had become buddies. Unbeknownst to them I was standing behind the door listening to their conversation. I heard Nana say, "Mandy is like her father. She needs a lot of attention. Please just be patient with her." I didn't know what she meant until years later.

Dropping the move to Virginia Beach on Nana was a shocker, but she knew I loved Kayla and would follow her anywhere. Five months after we moved Nana had a stroke. She always struggled with her weight and blood pressure. Something our black elders have always struggled with. I'm sure it was hereditary mixed with all her other vices, drinking, smoking, and a horrible diet. My cousin Nadiyah called me and said I should get back to New Jersey as quickly as possible. We made it back to New Jersey in time for me to see her in the hospital, but there was nothing the doctors could do. Her heart was strong but too much time had passed between her getting help and her brain not getting any oxygen. With Strokes it only takes a few minutes.

On January 19, 2002 Jean Doris Callender passed away. I watched as she was removed from life support just as I did my father. This time Kayla was in the room with me and my family and held my hand the entire time. No more Sunday dinners at Nana's house. It was like the scene from the Movie Soul Food. We all left the hospital distraught and in tears. Nana was the glue to the family and she was gone. The house had become a ghost town. No more climbing into the bed with her as I told her about my bad days and got head rubs. Even though I moved away no visit back home was complete without a trip to her house and lying in her bed underneath her. She basically took care of everyone. It became sink or swim for my uncles and cousins that were left living in the house after her death. Some swam. Some sank. I eventually learned that some unconditional love can be counter-productive. Some people use it as a crutch. You don't want to become an enabler. Giving unconditional love without accountability is not a good thing. Holding people accountable for their actions should not mean you don't love them. From what I remember my nana did the best she could raising her kids. I also learned that doing your best isn't always what is best. It's just what you know.

Her death was the beginning of my understanding that people aren't perfect. She wasn't perfect. We just place these fairy tale expectations on them then become so disappointed when they don't live up to them. She wasn't to everyone what she was to me. I'm fine with that. I used to ask her if she had favorites - kids or grandkids. She would say to me, "No, some just need more attention than others." I would only be left wondering how does a parent determine who needs more attention? And what happens to the kid that's receiving less attention? What happens to their outlook on love and life? Her death left me with more questions than answers.

GRANDMA

My grandma (maternal grandmother) was the strongest person I know. Not knew. I don't use past tense because I still have not met anyone that strong yet. She saved me and my siblings lives. She didn't wait until an accident or irreversible traumatic event to happen. She stepped in and took custody of us because she knew my mom wasn't capable all the time. She gave up her life to raise us. I watched her go to work for eight hours come home and make sure we had dinner and completed our homework, then she would go check on her own father that was living in a senior's building in another town. I made sure to be sitting on the porch when she came home from work. She looked so tired, but never once complained. I was always so happy to see her.. She represented consistency for me. I could always count on my grandma as a kid well into my adult years. She always made sure we had everything we needed from my first memory until Alzheimer's robbed her of her own. Even when Alzheimer's racked her brain a pinch of her old self would shine through. I would visit her in the nursing home and she always asked if I was okay. "Do you need anything?" she would say in a shaky voice.

"No Grandma, I'm fine," I would say as I rubbed her silver hair. It wasn't gray it was silver. She was nick named The Silver Fox by her friends. Grandma had a lot of friends and church family.

I learned so much just by watching her. I learned how to manage money. I learned how to speak to people respectfully. Most of all, I learned how to pray. She was so hard on us about everything; our education, appearance, and who we called friends. I needed her emotionally more times than not. I'm not sure if she had been so strong that she couldn't provide the emotional support. Sarah provided structure which in turn gave me an external shell that protects me through life's storms. She helped me build an emotional guard that allows me to ward off any vulnerabilities. Maybe it's why I hate being vulnerable, who knows; but I am her in so many ways.

Grandma had a strong personality and whatever she didn't agree with or like was stupid or strange. I think it's why I hid my sexuality from her for so long. I remember once I dropped my driver's license in a well-known gay bar downtown Newark named Murphy's! The person that found it lived in my neighborhood and was nice enough to return it. I remember getting home from work the next day and grandma saying, "Monica returned your license."

"Did she?" I had asked shockingly.

"Yes." She continued, "I wondered where she got it from. You know she's strange."

"Strange Grandma?"

"Yes. She likes girls."

"No Grandma, I didn't know that."

I was lying. I knew. I ran into Monica the night before in Murphy's. If I ever thought about having a conversation with grandma about my sexuality those hopes were crushed after that comment. I didn't want her to think I was weird. Strange. It's bad enough I liked sugar in my grits. I remember the first time she saw me sprinkle my grits with sugar she looked at me shockingly and said in a stern voice, "Where did you get that mess from?" I was a kid. I didn't remember. I just know the sugar made the grits sweeter. A tad bit better, the sweetness made me smile.

My grandma kept us in church. Sunday School, bible study, choir rehearsal, you name it, we were there. I would have to attribute my strong religious foundation to her upbringing. If not for her I would have never wanted to know more about spirituality. If she didn't believe in anything else, she believed in God. Her faith was unshakable.

I remember as a kid and as an adult having moved back home hearing her pray in the middle of the night. I would have to use the bathroom around 3 o'clock am and hear her in the kitchen or living room wide awake. "Does she ever sleep?" I recall thinking. But as I would get closer, I could hear she was praying for me, for us. I totally understand Helen Baylor's song, "Praying Grandmother." As a matter of fact, I'm still getting by on those prayers. I didn't understand until I became a parent myself. Now in the wee hours when I can't sleep, I am up praying for my son and family. It's like she left breadcrumbs. We have a huge family Bible where she recorded births, deaths, and marriages.

Sometimes I flip through it whenever I want to feel the thin pages of the word of God between my fingers instead of tapping the app on my phone. (Technology can never replace a Bible.)

She left notes on the pages expressing her love for us and instructions to always know we could go to God for anything. She emphasized how we should take care of each other and always stay close.

The toughness is what shone through most for me. She was so tough I would think that sometimes she didn't like me. I knew she loved me. I felt loved. She hugged me and kissed me. She just never really told me she loved me. I didn't know how much I needed to hear the words until I got older. I had to go back to my younger self and console kid Amanda. I literally said, "See! She did love you." I am not sure why she was so tough. Trials and struggles don't make everyone smile much, I guess. I understand everything she meant to teach me in this moment and I'm so grateful. Everything I do is to make her proud.

Sarah Lee Williams passed away from Alzheimer's disease on November 18, 2004.

Cousin/Bestfriend

Nadiyah and I were first cousins. Her mom Sharon and my dad Irving were siblings. Her mom was the only girl of 6 boys that fiercely protected her and loved her dearly. My Aunt Sharon was beautiful.

Growing up Nadiyah and I didn't spend much time together. On the weekends I would visit Nana, I can't remember her being there too often. She spent a lot of time with her dad. It wasn't until her junior year in college that we became inseparable. I was spending a lot of time at my nana's because my dad stayed there, and my grandmother Sarah had what I deemed in my twenties were too many rules. I often crashed in Nadiyah's room. It didn't matter how old we were my grandmother had rules if you were going to live under her roof. I'm sure Nana had rules too, just seemed less stringent and didn't seem to apply to me because I didn't actually "live" there.

Whenever Diyah, as we affectionately called her, came home during the summer and on weekends, we would stay up all hours of the night talking. We talked about everything from what she wanted to do when she graduated, her getting her own place, to the women I was dating. I remember when she graduated from college like it was yesterday. She was the first person in our family to do so. I was so proud. Me, Nana, my brother, Uncle Jerry and Diyah's brothers drove down to Maryland and spent the weekend just laughing and having fun. That Sunday at the graduation we made sure Nana sat as close as possible.

We had great seats, but that didn't stop me from standing in my chair clapping and yelling when her name was called. My mind went back to our late-night conversations about her hopes, dreams and fears. I was so proud of her. Nadiyah lost her mom in high school so I knew how much this degree meant to her. She felt like she had something to prove to everyone. After graduation, she went to work for the city of Newark for a couple of months then moved on to work for the State of NJ for DYFCS. I remember her having a boyfriend or two over the years but nothing too serious. So, when we all found out she was pregnant with her daughter it was a real shocker.

My brother, uncles, and Nana were so disappointed. I remember being at work and getting a call in the middle of the day from my Uncle Jerry. He went on and on about how difficult it would be for her to be a single mom and how all her hard work in college would be in vain because she was pregnant. His exact words were, "She may as well throw the degree in the garbage." I was shocked and confused. She had already defied the odds. Making it out of the projects, putting herself through college and obtaining gainful employment. Now her degree was trash because she was pregnant? Not only did I disagree, but it was the most idiotic thing I had ever heard. I used to think that expressing your disagreement with an elder was considered disrespectful, so I hesitated a bit before I expressed my opinion. Of course Nadiyah did just fine. She had her daughter Kimani and I helped her move into her first apartment.

She too was a bit disappointed about the Virginia move, but on the other hand she was excited about coming to visit. She would drive six hours with Kimani to visit with these extravagant plans of going out to the night clubs and hanging out. She always would just end up laying in our bed all weekend relaxing or hanging out on the beach for a couple of hours. We talked about everything, or so I thought.

Over the years, I knew about all the guys she dated. This latest guy, Seth, I knew was from the streets as being a previous drug dealer. "How did you end up dating him?" I remember asking at the beginning of their courtship.

"Girl I don't know," she would say.

He was an okay guy to me. However, whenever we visited Diyah and he was around Kayla never would make eye contact with him. "There's something I just don't like about him," she would say on our drive home. "Something isn't right about him."

Once you look back on a tragic event. You kind of remember the Matrix moments. The moment a bird flew on your windowsill. A song on the radio. A specific smell. I think if we don't notice at the time it's because we aren't vibrating on high enough frequency in order to be tuned in. If we do notice, we overlook the signs. There are so many events I can look back on and remember the signs I missed leading up to that culminating point. What I also know is, that telling someone bad news is harder than receiving it.

I remember my phone ringing around 1:00am on December 8, 2009. "Seth killed Nadiyah!!" my sister-in-law frantically screamed in my ear as soon as I picked up the phone.

I didn't comprehend at first. "Where's Kimani?!" I screamed back.

"She's in the ambulance with your brother!" she shouted back through her crying.

"Well what about Ishmael? Where is Ishmael?!" I screamed over her crying.

"He's with them too," she said.

Seth killed Nadiyah and my brother was with Kimani and Ishmael? What the heck is going on? I thought. I had awakened my wife with my yelling on the phone. As I hung up, I looked back at her and we kind of stared at each other for what seemed like eternity but was more like four minutes. I was six hours away from New Jersey in Virginia in a tailspin at 1:00am!! I had Seth's number from previous times we talked and him begging me to ask Nadiyah to take him back. I called him barely able to speak through my crying and gasping for air. I got his voicemail. "Why would you do this?", I screamed into the phone and hung up. It wasn't until 10 minutes later my brother reached the hospital with the kids that I found out from Ishmael, Seth had taken his own life as well. Ishmael was Nadiyah's nephew that she took care of. She practically raised him. As he explained to me what happened, I could tell by his monotone voice that he was in shock.

Once I snapped out of it, I realized it was now up to me to call the other members of our family. I would first reach out to Kimani's dad, Nadiyah's brother Os, my uncle Jerry, then on down the line.

What the heck am I going to say? Kimani's dad picked up right away. "Are you effing serious", he yelled. "I'm on my way" was the last thing he said to me. He needed to go get his baby girl. Uncle Jerry didn't answer so I called Cousin Meg. Once she got past her shock she said, "I can't call my daddy with this; he will literally have a heart attack, I'm going to have to drive to his house." I was grateful. No one wants to hear that type of news over the phone. Okay so let me back up a bit.

Nadiyah ended up dating Seth Jordan for several years. He ended up being caught in various lies about other women and him still being involved in the drug dealing lifestyle. Like any woman tired of substandard treatment and constant lies, she decided to break up with him.

They went back and forth for over a year. She wanted to break it off, but he wanted the relationship to work. She moved on. He didn't. Some days Seth professed his undying love for her, other days he threatened her life. I knew he didn't want to break up, but I had no idea about the threats. After a couple of months apart she was able to move on. Not knowing what he was capable of Nadiyah kept her new relationship a secret. Only close friends and family knew of her new beau. She had reignited an old flame with a college sweetheart that lived in Maryland. As she became more and more distant shunning his advances Seth became more persistent. When she changed the locks, he climbed through the windows, he would wait outside her house for her to show up, even came to her job. He showed up at the place where she got her hair done professing his undying love to her friends there. Basically, anyone that would listen. It was becoming a bit too much. Something had to be done. Nadiyah told my brother who was in law enforcement of Seth's behavior in hopes of easing her growing fears. After what seemed like a productive conversation with Seth, my brother advised her things would get better. If they didn't, he advised her to file a restraining order. Seth promised my brother he would let the relationship go and leave Nadiyah alone, however, this was before he discovered she was seeing someone else.

Unfortunately, once he found out all hell broke loose within 24 hours. She dropped Kimani and Ishmael off at my brother's house on Friday for the weekend. She had an amazing time in Maryland until Sunday evening. Around 6pm Seth began calling her phone constantly rattling off irrational threats. Her and I spoke briefly before she headed back to New Jersey and she expressed her concerns over Seth's anger and an argument he had with her boyfriend over the phone. She hurried home thinking she would file the restraining order the first thing Monday morning like my brother had advised her. To make her feel a little better she even called me on the phone in route home to discuss the evening's nerve shattering events in detail. We talked off and on while she drove back to New Jersey to pick up the kids. I assured her Seth wouldn't do anything to harm her because he himself had a child of his own that he adored. I thought why would he do something stupid and end up in jail and not be able to see his kid? That was my rationale. "Seth has more sense than that," I joked. She responded with an uneasy laugh. This would be the last time I talked to my cousin.

On December 7, 2008 after picking up the kids from my brother, Nadiyah pulled up to her house around 11:30pm. As she parked the car, she noticed Seth sitting in his truck at the end of the block with the lights out. She called me immediately to express her concern, but I was asleep. I would later listen to the voicemail she left expressing her angst about getting out of the car. Panic stricken she rushed the kids in the house dropping her keys along the way. As she picked up her keys and gathered her things, he was upon her, asking question after question regarding her whereabouts that weekend.

Nervously, she tried to answer his questions without getting him more upset. He forced his way in the house with her and her children ordering them into their rooms. He shoved her into the bedroom, slamming the door behind them so she couldn't escape his rage and barrage of never-ending questions. They argued for several minutes until her nephew heard her yell, "Call the cops." Then she screamed, "We can work this out!"

Then the kids heard several loud pops as Ishmael called the cops and my brother who was just reporting to his night shift at the time. "I'm on my way", said my brother who worked at a local police precinct. During the seven minutes it took for the police to arrive there was silence. Once my brother entered the house, he approached the closed bedroom door. He had his partner standing outside the bedroom window in case Seth tried to make a run for it. He kicked the bedroom door open to see Nadiyah and Seth, both dead, covered in blood.

From regular officer to Superman, he whisked the kids away from the scene in hopes of preventing them the anguish of seeing what his eyes couldn't believe. Seth had taken Nadiyah's life and his own in the wee hours of December 8, 2008. With no regard for anyone other than himself he took away a mother, sister, aunt, daughter, cousin, niece, and great friend to many. In several minutes he changed the dynamics of many lives, especially the children that heard the deathly turn of events.

My family will forever be haunted by this tragedy not only because of the heinous nature of the crime, but because her cousin, my brother, was the first officer on the scene.

No one can say what Seth's motives were or begin to understand what drove him to commit such a brutal act. No one knows why domestic violence shatters lives daily. What could Diyah have done differently? Would the piece of paper known as a "restraining order" had saved her life? I think not, but we will never know.

Preparing to head back to Virginia after Nadiyah's services was heart wrenching. I felt like I was leaving a piece of me behind, not to mention her beautiful daughter Kimani. Who will take care of her? What will happen to her belongings? My brain felt like mush and my heart was in tiny pieces. Even though in our conversations Nadiyah would say if something ever happened to her for me to please take care of Kimani. She even made sure I was the beneficiary of her life insurance policy. However, there was nothing in writing. You can't go to court with a conversation as your evidence and expect it to hold up.

After a conversation with my brother he convinced me it was in Kimani's best interest that she stays with him and his wife. He didn't want her routine to change after such a tragic event by moving to Virginia with me. I didn't want to get into an argument with him let alone legal battle, especially at a time like this. I was offended. What could they provide that we couldn't?! I could barely look at Kimani without crying let alone drag my brother into a court room. I reassured myself she would be fine with him. My emotions were all over the place. I had to pull it together; at least that's what I kept telling myself.

We said our goodbyes, climbed into the car and drove for what seemed like my entire life down the New Jersey Turnpike. Everything was a blur. Exit after exit, on to Delaware, Maryland and into Virginia. Time seemed to have slowed down. Somehow a normally six-hour drive dragged on for eight hours. Finally, we were home. I went in the house and lay down just as I did when my mom passed away.

However, this time I didn't get up for several weeks. No. Really, I did not get out of the bed. I couldn't move.

My wife cooked for me, she kept the house up, some days she even bathed me. I was in a daze. I felt so sad and empty. When I did go back to work, my mind was someplace else. The country had elected the first Black President. It felt like everyone everywhere was excited except me. Diyah and I talked on the phone back in November as we were going to vote. I told her about the long lines that were in Virginia and she talked about the excitement in Newark. Nadiyah would never get to see Obama's Presidency. Hell, at the time I didn't care. I just wanted my cousin back. Spring and summer came and went, and I barely noticed. Just as summer was ending, I was hit with more bad news.

NEPHEW

It was the Spring of 2005. "He's here," Diyah's voice said over the phone after I picked it up on the third ring.

"Well, you have to go and see him since I'm not there. Make sure he's ours," I said jokingly.

"Ours?" she questioned.

"Yes!" I said as I proceeded to tell her the story Nana told me about when I was born. "Nana said she went to the hospital the day I was born and as she peeked in the nursery my mom asked, 'Can you guess which one she is?' Nana said she pointed at me without hesitation, with my bald head and pink lips saying, 'That one right there is ours,' meaning, a Callender. She had picked me out from behind the nursery glass full of crying babies without looking at the name tags." Nadiyah laughed at me so hard but was very dismissive. She would eventually make it to see Kindel, but not until weeks later. By now, Kindel's mom and my brother were broken up. The one visit was it for Diyah. Her loyalty lied with my brother. "Fine," I remember saying as I hung up the phone. "I will come up and see myself." My loyalty was with what was the right thing to do. It's how I was raised. And that was not to deny or disregard a baby that was my blood. A Callender boy.

I remember pacing back and forth in Diyah's living room anticipating their arrival. Not only would this be my first-time meeting Kindel I had never met his mother Cassie either.

I suggested we meet at Diyah's house because she at least knew her, and I wanted Cassie to be comfortable. I was a total stranger to her. Nadiyah was on her way to a wedding hardly paying me any attention. Her main concerns were which shoes she should wear and whether to pin her hair up or wear it down. Once they arrived, Diyah introduced us and continued around the house getting ready for her event. Cassie sat next to me on the sofa then sat the car seat on the floor.

It was summertime so she had a light linen cover protecting his face from the bugs as she walked from the car. She pulled it back and gently lifted him out and handed him to me. It was then that I realized I didn't have Nana's superpowers. He looked just like his mom who was beautiful by the way. She nervously repeatedly moved her hair from her eyes as she watched me intently as I kissed his hands and rubbed his head. "Wow," I heard her say in a low voice. "You look just like your brother."

"Yes, we have strong genes," I replied. My eyes darted between her and Kindel back and forth back and forth for about five minutes. I finally broke the silence in the room and said, "So, this is my nephew huh?"

She nodded and said, "Yes."

I replied, "Do you know what I'm sacrificing by being here?" She didn't answer. She just stared at him. As usual, I looked over at my wife for a sign that I was doing the right thing.

She rubbed my back as I just stared at him. "Let me hold him," Kayla said.

Cassie stayed for about an hour, we exchanged numbers and she was off on her way. As soon as the door closed Nadiyah immediately said. "Your brother is going to kill you."

Death may have been easier. My brother was so angry that we didn't speak for about a year. In that year Cassie and I kept in touch and became great friends. I saw Kindel whenever I came to town. She even visited us in Virginia Beach or allowed us to take him back with us whenever we wanted.

I was raised to do the right thing and not the loyal or popular thing. One of my hardest lessons would be the right thing isn't always the popular choice and sometimes you will stand alone. I would rather stand alone and be able to sleep at night than roll with the punches and not be able to look at myself in the mirror. Then again, some people can do some shady stuff and sleep very well at night.

We filled a void in each other's lives. My wife and I wanted a baby badly at the time and Cassie was a single parent. She allowed us to be in his life as more than Aunties. I felt like we were co parents. We got daily pictures, emails, phone calls, and an abundance of visits. It felt like my presence was protecting him from some ugly truth. People think babies and kids don't notice absences. It may be true you can't miss what you never had, but I was going to make damn sure he didn't get a chance to feel unwanted or feel like a mistake. There was something about the innocence in his wide bright smile.

Fast forward four years later. Summer had just ended, and it was a nice warm morning in Virginia Beach in September of 2009. Things were better between my brother and Cassie, but I still hadn't adjusted to life without Nadiyah, although I was doing my best. I missed our morning calls before we started our day. No matter what type of morning she was having she always said, "Good Morning Sunshine," as soon as I picked up the phone.

One morning I was heading home from dropping Kayla off at work when I received a call from my brother. He sounded very angry. He just kept yelling, "What the heck?" What the heck?" I knew something was wrong, so I pulled over to talk to him. He just screamed, "My son is dead!"

I got lightheaded as I dared part my lips to ask which one? He had three adorable sons and my heart just couldn't take losing any one of them. All that would come out of my mouth was, "huh?"

Then he yelled his name, "KINDEL!"

I didn't understand because Kindel, his mom and her fiancé had just visited us in Virginia the weekend before. I calmly said, "I will call you back," and hung up the phone.

I called Kindel's mom and once she heard my voice she just moaned. It was like she had a horrible pain that wouldn't subside. I knew now that she couldn't talk, and she didn't have to. The pain had taken her voice. I calmly said. "Okay, okay, you don't have to say anything." I wasn't a mom at the time, but you couldn't tell me Kindel wasn't our son as well. From the time he was three months old and I held him in my arms he was my son too. I told her whatever she needed me to do I would do it. Just let me know. After we hung up, it hit me that I would have to drive back to my wife's job and give her the devastating news. This was her baby too. I slowly drove back to her office searching for the words to use. When I went inside, I asked her supervisor if we could use the conference room for a family emergency. I sat there with my head down as they brought her in. Here I was having to deliver bad news again. This time in person.

When she saw me, she sensed something was wrong. It was in that moment as I tried to look away at the paintings on the wall, I realized I had never been inside her job. There was no need for me to even tell her to sit down. I just hit her with it. "Hun... Kindel died." The look on her face was like I was speaking Russian. Spanish you can kind of decipher, but the look on her face was pure confusion and denial. I just stared at her because I couldn't repeat the words again. She immediately screamed and burst into tears. She didn't ask any questions just as I hadn't of Kindel's mom. We just knew he was gone.

September 29, 2009 Kindel Fleming Robinson tragically drowned. He was four years old. He would have been a Veterinarian. He loved animals. From the time he was six months old his mom would let us bring him back to Virginia for visits whenever we wanted. If we weren't in town and wanted to see him, we would do what we termed a "halfway." Technically it's a six hour drive down the Eastern Shore from NJ to Virginia Beach. A halfway is considered both of us driving three hours and meeting in Delaware, have lunch, then Kayla and I would take him.

We did the same thing when it was time for him to go back home. I never thought about the amount of trust she had to have in us to allow her only son to not just stay with us but out of the state for days at a time.

It was an honor and a privilege. We did everything together when he was in town. There are no appropriate words when you must bury a child. That void in my heart still exists, however I see so much of him in my son Jax. It's a reminder that angels are real.

Big Dad

Bonus Dad…I made that up while writing this book. That was Lacy Sr. My brother Lacy's dad and my mother's husband. His love and influence will not be diminished by referring to him as a "step-father." He was more than that. He was my Bonus Dad. His presence didn't allow me to miss my dad Irving much. Bonus is something welcome and often unexpected that accompanies and enhances a thing that is good. Our life was good, but he came along and enhanced it. To be honest I don't remember my life before him. I think I was around six years old when he married my mom. He's been my dad since then. He made sure we had school clothes, took us to amusement parks, taught me how to ride a bike, and play poker. He met all my boyfriends and girlfriends. He chauffeured my oldest sister Steffi to her prom and was at all my karate tournaments, even though I wasn't good at it. Big Dad taught me about sports and was instrumental in my love for football and baseball. The NY Giants and the NY Mets were his favorite teams and naturally became mine.

I watched him show my mother love and respect even after they had separated, which shaped my view on how a man is supposed to treat a woman. Even when he and my mom separated, he never stopped being present in our lives. On weekends when he picked up my brother Lacy Jr. we always had the option to go. Whenever I did, we would spend long summer nights in the backyard or basement of his parents' home. My third set of grandparents. Nana and Poppi Preston.

He would drive my grandma food shopping; he made sure my nephew Kenyour (Steffi's son) got weekly haircuts when he took Lacy Jr. and he made sure we had pocket change. I remember when I first moved to Virginia and didn't have a job. I checked the mail one day and there was a $100 money order from him.

Big Dad is what we affectionately called him. He was the neighborhood Big Dad. He was my Santa Claus and superhero. He made sure our faces were lit up on Christmas day and soothed my broken hearts. "Do you want me to kick his butt?" he would jokingly say whenever he thought I was sad about a guy. Lacy Sr was my protector and provider. There was nothing I didn't think he couldn't do. He and my mother had moved on in their lives at the time of her death yet never divorcing. He stood by us to bury her, revisiting the church pews we grew up in as kids. I don't think I have ever met a stronger, more loving, giving man. They say a girl's first love is her dad, well he was mine. He was my first love.

The second would be a guy that reminded me of him so much. Not just in stature, but his good looks and personality as well.

I think I looked for him in every guy I dated until realizing I'm just going to strictly date women. Maybe in some inexplicable way since I couldn't find him in a man, I became him as a woman. Meaning I became the protector, provider, head of household of my family. No, I have no desire to be a man, but I think I took on his personality. That nature verses nurture is real thing. What man meets and marries a woman with three children from three different men, marries her and takes care of those children like his own? You don't come across men like him anymore. My father Lacy Preston Sr. passed away on December 5, 2010.

I made it to the rehab facility where he died just as the funeral home was arriving to pick up his body. My brother was crying his eyes out in the parking lot. I had never seen Lacy Jr crying so hard since we were kids. He went to my mother's wake but opted out of her funeral. I briefly consoled Lacy Jr, then went upstairs to Big Dad's room. There he was laying so peaceful. My Big Dad. My hero was gone. His funeral was in the same church as Nadiyah's funeral. Here

I was two years later in the same front pew in the same suit crying my eyes out again.

So, there you have it. My grief. My pain. My angst. My despair. Death rings your doorbell and invites itself to dinner. It pushes past you standing in the doorway before you can say, "There isn't enough to go around." Then it takes bits and pieces of your heart as leftovers in your good Tupperware, never to return it. Between my parents, grandmothers, my cousin, and nephew I had no Tupperware left. I had nothing to give. Death and grief didn't care. I was an empty shell of my former self. I could not believe that my loved ones were dying right before my eyes. A few of them literally. I felt so helpless. Mainly Hopeless.

"Sorrows are our best educators. One can see further through a tear than a telescope."

—Lord Byron [3]

CHAPTER 5

Get Up Girl

My mom used to say depression was a luxury black people couldn't afford. That's one of the things I miss about her most. She always had a sarcastic witty saying ready to fire off at any minute. Sort of like me. Can you imagine being too poor to even be sad? Wow. Let me rephrase that. You could be sad and poor; you just couldn't afford to take the time from work. I would see movies where white wealthy people would take months even years from work because they were grieving, sad, or depressed. Everyone isn't that lucky. As fate would have it, I lost my job in January 2009, a month after Nadiyah's murder. Looking back, it was perfect timing. I didn't know how long I would be able to continually drag myself into the office feeling totally empty. I laid in the bed for weeks after being fired. It was painful to get out of bed. My wife fed me, washed me, and even dressed me. I could barely lift my hands above my head. Some days she allowed me to stay in bed and she would open the window for air and the blinds for sunshine. Some days she dressed me and sat me on the porch with the dog in hopes of me taking him for a walk. I was basically in a daze.

I ended up taking a year off work. Trust me it wasn't intentional, nor was I wealthy. They gave me a great severance package and I just didn't have it in me mentally to look for another job. The day they let me go, the company I was working for sent two managers from the corporate office to deliver me the bad news. We sat there for about 30 minutes exchanging friendly banter until I had enough. "Okay guys, what's this really about?" I asked as my tone changed. "Well Amanda," one manager said. UHS just doesn't have a position for you in the new direction that the company is going." I just nodded and said, "Okay."

Apparently, the years of driving back and forth from New Jersey to Virginia I had accumulated a lot of speeding tickets. I had 11 points on my driver's license. "Wow and Damn girl," are a few things that came to mind as I watched their lips moving. But I already knew this. The company was moving towards the rental side of medical equipment. I would have to deliver and pick up the equipment, however their new auto insurance carrier wouldn't insure me. So they had to let me go. I was relieved. I had been doing my best to hold it together. Visions of Nadiyah's casket going into the ground repeatedly played in my mind. I held it together the entire funeral, but that moment I lost my composure. My uncle Tony had to hold me up. I couldn't get the vision of the uncontrollable shaking Cassie's body did as she watched Kindel's body being lowered into the ground at his burial.

I could barely focus on work. I'm sure they thought I was going to lose it in the parking lot. Contrarily, I didn't feel a thing. I welcomed the unexpected hiatus from work. The time off went by so fast. The year felt like a month. In that time, I learned so much about myself, my pain, and how to handle grief. Well, you don't "handle" grief. It comes in waves like in the Atlantic Ocean. So, I guess it's safe to say I managed it. Or better yet, I learned to surf. However, even the best surfers experience a wipeout from a killer wave from time to time. Sure, enough that's how I felt. Like a giant wave have overtaken me and I just couldn't move my arms to swim anymore. I was wiped out.

Drowning in a sea of melancholy emotions I went to therapy a month after Kindel's death. Wait, as usual I'm making this sound way too easy. What really happened was one night about a week after I was fired, I was home alone. Out of nowhere I suddenly felt extremely overwhelmed with sadness. The room got dark and cold and I felt like my soul was leaving my body. I couldn't move. Tears slowly streamed down my face, but I couldn't move my hands to wipe them away. As I stared off into nothingness the sadness had enveloped my entire being. I almost couldn't breathe. Grief had taken over my entire body and I felt like death was coming for me. However, I didn't want to sit around and wait for it. Years later I would recognize these signs again as having an anxiety attack, but in that moment, I just knew I was dying. What felt like hours later, my body emptied from all the tears, I managed to feel my heartbeat again. In that moment I knew I didn't want to die.

I called a crisis hotline. This was one time being vulnerable didn't matter. Maybe it's because I was talking to a stranger, I'm not sure. I just know I didn't want to die. I was having a mental health crisis right in the middle of my living room floor alone. So, this is what a nervous breakdown sort of feels like....like death. Someone talked to me for about 30 minutes until I felt better then recommended some therapists in the area. It was considered an emergency so the first therapist I chose was able to see me the next day. I don't remember sleeping much that night. I just remember waking up so tired.

As soon as I walked into the therapist office, I felt very comfortable with her. Her office was warm and inviting. She was very understanding and not condescending, knowledgeable, but not a know it all. She looked at me as if she could tell I had been crying all night. Like she could tell immediately that I was broken. Was there a sign on my forehead?! Once I talked about my life during the first session, she couldn't understand how I had gone this long without getting some emotional support. I'm not sure if it's against protocol for therapists to hug patients, but she asked me was it okay if she gave me a hug. Apparently, it looked like I needed one after explaining to her loss after loss after loss.

I'm sure I went over the allotted time. She let me go on and on and through every single emotion, until I was hoarse, and all cried out. After that initial visit getting to know each other, we started with a schedule of one day a week. She was great. Finding the right therapist is detrimental to recovering from grief. Over the next couple months in therapy I realized I couldn't outrun the pain. I needed to FEEL the feelings. I had packed away the pain after each death until my body couldn't contain the emotions anymore. I never stopped to let my emotions flow. It's like I was backed up. I needed an emotional enema. My therapist let me cry hard and often. I felt like she had a new box of tissues during every session especially for me. I felt real low for a very long time, like I was in a valley. Valleys are low areas between hills or mountains typically with a river running through it. However, I didn't feel like there was a river. I just felt low, dry, and alone. I knew something was wrong, but I didn't have the emotional bandwidth to do anything about it. Therapy saved my life.

Being so sad and in pain I started to question where God was in all of this. Where is the big guy? Doesn't he see how much I'm hurting? I would find myself looking up at the sky from time to time expecting his arms to magically descend from the clouds and scoop me up with a big hug. Where was the savior that my grandmother promised would never let me down? She told me I could always count on him. I thought he would recognize my pain and send in the cavalry. Why is he letting me suffer like this? As a kid hearing bible stories, I always pictured God as a white guy with perfect skin and hair that sat on top of the clouds dispensing judgment on sinners, healing the sick and lifting people from bad times.

You all know what I'm talking about. That miracle worker guy! Where was he? Come out come out wherever you are!! I needed him now more than ever, but I didn't sense his presence. When I didn't feel him; I picked a fight with him. I thought if I poked him like a bear he would show up. My mom used to say, "It takes two people to argue." Maybe God himself coined that phrase because he never responded. It was always silence. Things I wouldn't dare say to my parents out of respect I hurled at God in anger.

Maybe if I disrespected him, he would reveal himself to me I naively thought. I would go to the oceanfront or a lake and have these emotional one sided, knock down drag out arguments. Well.... conversations. I would curse him for my anguish and beg for help in the same breath. I was angry and desperate. For some reason I always went to argue with him near water. Who gets dressed to go pick a fight with GOD? Me, that's who!! Maybe I just wanted to go in the water and never come out. I'm not sure. I can't say for certain that I never thought about taking my life. Maybe I wanted to die. If I tried to kill myself will he then show up and save me from the clutches of grief? I'm not sure how I felt. I just wanted the pain to stop. I would fall to my knees in the wet sand or dirt, face filled with tears and agony in my voice begging for answers. "Why God; why?!" I would scream. However, there was always silence. "How could you let this happen?!" I would yell. I was so disappointed in him.

Okay so my parents were addicts, fine! My grandmothers and Big Dad had health issues, I got it. These are the realities I could handle about their deaths. "But God you snatched away Nadiyah and Kindel so brutally and so tragically!" I screamed. "She was my best friend and he was just a kid. Why God? Why?" The hole in my heart was unbearable and I thought I deserved answers. There was always silence, nothing but SILENCE.

Finally, after months of interrogation, anger and a few insults. (Yes, I insulted God.) I stopped speaking to him. The line had been drawn in the sand. I stopped praying, I stopped acknowledging him, I put my Bible in the nightstand drawer, and I stopped going to church. I put him on knock off. I turned my back on God. He was a fraud in my eyes. Silly religion only works during good times, I thought at my last attempt.

I hobbled on with whatever shell of an existence I had at the time. I spent days in my room sinking deeper and deeper into depression. Even with therapy I was still so sad. I was getting angrier, jaded and gaining weight. Some days it hurt just to get out of bed. I felt so alone. If my therapist was so great, why was I still so sad? My thoughts reverted to Diyah's murder and the emptiness it left inside of me. Missing someone on an extended vacation or away on a work assignment you can look forward to the day when you will see them again no matter how long. However, missing a dead person opens this gaping hole in your heart that never closes. You spend time searching for memories in the corners of your mind just for a few moments of relief from the pain. Memories of Diyah were different though. I rarely thought of a happy memory. Instead my mind went back to her murder and the days afterwards. I guess this was me searching for a "why" again. Trying to relive moments to see what I could have done to save her.

I thought back to the drive to New Jersey the morning after her death. After the 1am phone call and alerting my other relatives I managed to go back to sleep. Only to wake up a couple of hours later realizing it wasn't a dream. My cousin and best friend was dead. It took me a long time to say she was murdered. I was in shock for months.

I couldn't believe she was gone. We talked every day. Even on days she was angry with Kimani for making her late for work, or tired from being on call overnight, she made sure to call me. These memories bounced around my brain as I got dressed to head back to New Jersey. As we were leaving, I remembered to call my sister Steffi who lived in Virginia Beach by now. Before I could hang up, she said, "I'm not letting you go alone." We picked her up and as she climbed into the car, I realized how happy I was to have her there.

I always drive on road trips. Let me rephrase that. I drive everywhere. It's a thing. I just don't trust other folks driving. This time I just let my wife take the wheel as I sat in the front seat staring aimlessly out the window. Normally on our road trips to New Jersey, we blast music and talk about things we are going to do once we get to town. Not this trip. I can't remember if we even played the radio. All I remember is a heavy silence and periodic crying. Once we got to New Jersey and settled in at my brother's house I was tasked with making Nadiyah's funeral arrangements. She and I talked about everything. Including the dreaded if I die conversations. However, I never imagined I would have to do it. When I went through her house with two of her siblings it wasn't a memory collecting mission for me. I was there to find her life insurance policy, bank records, and any clue on how to handle her personal business before heading back home to Virginia.

We pulled up to Diyah's house and I could see a woman sitting on the porch crying. I didn't recognize her but she stood up to greet me as I exited the car. She introduced herself as Seth's sister and began to apologize profusely. I can't remember her name, but she was visibly shaken and remorseful. I don't' remember what I said to her, but I do know she is the only person in his family that made contact with me and apologized. I can't speak for anyone else in my family.

It had only been 24 hours since the murder and let's just say cleaning up a crime scene is not the job description of the police. It took everything in me to walk through her house. My brother on the other hand understandably sat in the car. However, as always there was Kayla right by my side. I took a deep breath and put the key in the door. I found what I was looking for in about an hour in her bedroom where she had been killed. I imagined her in that space in her final minutes. How terrified she had to have been. It was then I said to myself I must see her before the funeral. I want to see my cousin right now, I thought. I called the funeral home I had chosen to make the arrangements and said, "Don't touch her until I see her. I want to know what happened here." I walked from the bedroom, through the living room, to the kitchen. It was eerily quiet. I ran my hands across the furniture and remembered all the days I was in town and spent in that house. Eating, napping, laughing, hell, I remember helping her move in! It was in that very living room where my wife and I met Kindel for the first time. I was so excited. Nadiyah was on her way to a wedding and as we waited for Kindel's mom I told her how pretty she looked. She smiled and said, "Take my picture." We had no idea that picture would end up on the cover of her funeral program. There were many good memories in that house. I found her cell phone and listened to some of the voice messages. Distraught person after distraught person was calling her in denial, wanting to hear her voice.

Everyone was hoping this was some other Nadiyah Johnson. I put the phone in my pocket and decided I had enough. I didn't want to let the horror of what happened taint my memory, so I grabbed a couple of pictures for Kimani and left everyone else to take what they wanted. My heart couldn't do it anymore. As I walked out and looked up briefly to wipe my tears there it was. The little black Toyota Solara that she loved so much. I remember when she first purchased it, she called me on the phone to haggle with the salesman. She called me when she got oil changes and they tried to talk her into imaginary repairs for other things. LOL!! We know how those places are. She thought I could fix everything.

God why couldn't I fix this?! I couldn't save her! I would call the bank to come pick it up from my brother's house, but until then I was going to drive it. I hopped in alone and played whatever CD was in and cried the entire 45-minute trip back to my brother's house. Looking back my only regret is not getting more keepsakes for Kimani. The next day I went to clean out her desk at her job and a slew of her friends and coworkers greeted me. Some I knew of from our daily conversations and some I didn't. The ones I didn't know just wanted to express their sadness and disbelief. Wow, she was loved I thought as person after person insisted on hugging me. What also blew my mind was they all knew me. "You must be Amanda," the ones that didn't know me said. "Your cousin talked about you all the time." After that was done a day or two later, we had an appointment with the funeral home to make the arrangements.

My Uncle Jerry, my brother, Kayla, Ishmael, and myself sat around that table for hours planning her services. Every detail had to be perfect for our Princess. We were there so long they ordered us lunch. I spared no expense. Well she spared no expense. She was financially prepared. Not too many people are. She was very responsible in that aspect. After that daunting task was complete, I said, "Okay

I'm ready." The funeral director stood up from the meeting table and asked whether I was sure. Her body had just come from the medical examiner's office and he hadn't had time to clean her up. "I'm sure," I said as I swallowed hard. "I need to see her so I can instruct you on how she's supposed to look." He assured me that a picture would do. However, something in my gut needed to see her. My brother wanted no parts after finding her the way he did. My uncle Jerry looked at me and said, "Well I'm not going to let you do it alone." I looked at my wife who added, "Neither am I." Poor Ishmael just got caught up in the moment. I think he was least prepared for what we were about to see.

As we walked down to the winding staircase to the room where her body was, I could feel my legs go numb, my hands get sweaty, and my heart started to beat fast. The room wasn't too big, so we didn't have far to walk. It seemed more grey than dark, which added to the sadness that had begun to tighten my chest. I'm not sure if a light was just shining on her or that's how I felt. As I slowly walked across the room, I could feel the others immediately behind me. I can't remember anything else in the room, because my eyes were fixed upon her. I wanted to grab her, lift her and just run out the door with her. As I stood over her body, I paused briefly, took a deep breath, and then nodded for the funeral director to pull the sheet back. There she was. My best friend. I just stood there tears running down my face. The funeral director began to explain to us what we were seeing in terms of the wounds. I could hear my uncle behind me gasping. "OH MY GOD," he blurted out. I never flinched. I could hear Ishmael crying behind me as well. I heard a slight sniffle from my wife, as I felt her squeeze my hand.

Diyah was shot multiple times in the torso and arm, breaking the bone. However, that's not what killed her. This animal put the gun to the back of her head and pulled the trigger. The bullet exited through her forehead, cracking her skull in pieces. There was my beautiful cousin laying there with her head in pieces. Suddenly I began to silently cry. Soon after I heard and felt myself physically weeping. My body shook as each emotion exited my body.

My body literally got warm and it seemed my shirt became two sizes too small from holding in my emotional explosion. I slowly reached out, my hand visibly shaking and touched her cheeks, she was so so cold. I said, "No, No, No! You must fix her. Her daughter cannot see her like this." I've dealt with other funeral homes in the past and let's just say they hadn't done the best job. If you can't fix her. I'm not opening the casket. I kept using the word fix. I'm not sure but maybe in my mind if she looked like her beautiful self then this monster didn't win after all. The funeral director assured me that he could make her look like sleeping beauty. I told him, "Do it please." I kissed her ice-cold cheeks and vowed to come back before the services to ensure she was indeed sleeping beauty. I could have sat there for hours, just staring at her. Hurt, denial, and disbelief had taken up residence in my body. I'm sure everyone was relieved when I finally took two steps back and motioned for him to place the white sheet back over her face.

Every so often I would shake off the image and just shake my head no. This can't be real. Most people would think I'm insane for wanting to see her like that. It's just how I process things. It's what makes things final for me. It's where I can cry in peace aside from the gawking of a public viewing.

Especially this one that I figured would be especially crowded. The following days consisted of writing her obituary, finding her a burial outfit and awaiting other relatives arriving from out of town. It was a homicide so of course it made the local newspaper, The Star Ledger. I could not believe some of the comments that people were making. I vowed to never read the comments ever again and pray that Kimani never ever saw them. How someone manages to blame the victim in domestic violence is beyond me. When did everyone become an expert on these situations? What made me feel sicker is because of their last names the newspaper had their obituaries next to each other.

He killed her. I didn't think he deserved anything, but a fiery seat in hell.

The day before the services I received the call from the funeral home to preview her body and drop off her outfit. Same as before my uncle Jerry and wife made the trek down the winding stairs of the funeral home with me. This time, our gasps weren't from shock. These people had done an amazing job. Then it hit me. Nadiyah was dead and her funeral was tomorrow. I cried openly and loudly this time. I leaned in on her and gave her the biggest hug ever. The funeral director appeared with tissue. As he slid me the tissue trying not to disturb me, I slightly squeezed his hand. It was my nonverbal thank you.

During the services she looked like she was asleep. I had them rope off the casket so no one outside of family would touch her. I'm forever grateful for their work. I remember pulling up to the church and seeing a line of people that filtered out the church down the block. So many people waited in line for hours to see her and pay their respects. During her wake I didn't sit still too much. If I did, I was in a daze, staring and crying. I didn't want some stranger consoling me although I'm sure everyone meant well. Every so often I would I stand in the back of the church taking it all in. Hoping and praying everything was to her approval. This is the memory that constantly played in my head. She was loved. After the viewing before she was eulogized, I walked up to the casket, reached in and kissed her cheek for the last time.

"You can let her tragic death destroy
you or her legacy inspire you."

—Traci Callender

Each time I searched for God during all of this and I couldn't find him. Each time I became angrier and angrier. Every day my thoughts went from the sadness and emptiness of missing Diyah and Kindel to anger at my parents. Each time trying to scrounge up any memory of my parents that didn't evoke resentment. Whenever my wife caught me in a daze, she would rub my head and reassure me everything would be okay. Even if I was angry with God, I always knew my wife loved and trusted him. I was riding on her coattail of faith so to speak. On the days I would decline to attend church with her she would smirk and say, "Still not speaking to him huh?!" I never answered her. I would get so angry at her for not jumping on the band wagon with me. Doesn't she see what he's done to my life? I wondered. He took away two of the people that helped me breathe.

Then it hit me. That's it. I couldn't breathe!! There I said it. There was an elephant standing on my chest and talking to a therapist every other week wasn't easing the pain as fast as I had hoped. Surely, she was holding out on waving her magic wand and making everything better. Why was she making me work so hard?! Spoiler alert, if you have ever been to therapy there is no liquor bottle in the desk drawer or a magic wand to wave. It consists of good ole fashioned hard work.

My therapist decided to work on the feelings I could change and that was the anger towards my parents. I would always have good and bad days surrounding the sadness of a tragedy; however, I needed to address the resentment that lived in me regarding my parents.

On the advice of my therapist, I began to write letters to my mom. I told her how angry I was. How hurt I was. How much I missed her. Everything I ever wanted to say to her I wrote down. Whether it was a childhood secret or a forgotten feeling of longing. I cried a lot. Initially I hated that I cried so much and would try and stop.

The spigot of tears would flow at the most inopportune times. Did I mention I hate being vulnerable? I would be in the line at the grocery store or in the drive through just crying. Can you imagine asking for extra for ketchup for your fries with tears rolling down your face?! I can only imagine what folks thought. I figured, the employees of these establishments wanted to yell, "Girl the ketchup is free! Wipe your face!" LOL! And most times it wasn't just single tears. I was out in these streets boo hoo'ing and I had no idea why. Then I discovered the tears were a way for the pain to leave my body. I would feel so much better after a good cry.

Eventually I stopped trying to prevent the tears. I just let them flow. My body exploded and all the emotions were oozing out via my tears. My favorite place to cry became the shower. I could be in there for hours crying and the tears would flow down my face and down the drain with the rest of the water. If I sobbed it was muffled by the sound of the water cascading off the walls. I quickly realized I wasn't just crying about missing Nadiyah and Kindel. This was old hurt resurfacing and exiting my body.

This was the hurt I was trying not to acknowledge for so many years. All the emotions I had managed to hold at bay over the years were finally exploding like a volcano. It was like I was back in sixth grade again on stage in my school play, looking out into the sea of parents expecting to see one of my parents' faces and them not being there. This was those tears I held back. Watching my mom get high in front of me. And I don't mean smoking a joint get high. These were those tears I held back. Not getting phone calls from my dad on my birthdays. I always pretended I didn't care. Apparently, I did. These were those tears I held back. The times I visited my nana on weekends looking forward to seeing my dad and him not being there. Didn't he miss me? These were those tears I held back. My dad laying in the hospital and asking me to bring him drugs. Did he say what I think he said? These were those tears I held back. This was compounded grief.

The grief that I never dealt with had continued to fill up inside of me like grain in a silo. I couldn't cope because I hadn't healed from past events. Things just kept piling up over time finally spiraling out of control with the loss of Diyah and Kindel.

Allowing myself to feel these emotions brought so many moments of clarity and questions. What were my parents trying to escape or forget in their addiction and why? What traumas or pain were drugs and alcohol numbing for them? In that moment it all became relatable, because I most certainly wanted to take something to make my pain stop. I thought, did they have the same feelings which led to their addiction? I wanted something to take me out of the moment because the feelings were so painful.

Drugs. Alcohol. Anything. Maybe there was something they too were trying to forget or emotionally escape from.

I believe we inherit negative characteristics and preferences from our parents and are prone to pass them to our kids. Once it starts to negatively affect our lives and people around us it can be said to be a generational curse. That's what this was. The pain and remnants of addiction, anxiety, trauma and poverty seemed to be strongholds that were passing through generations of my family. My uncle had told me stories about his father, my grandfather doing drugs. Previous generations never addressed the issues they had, they only self-medicated with alcohol, drugs and other self-damaging behavior and neglected whatever didn't serve that purpose. You don't just live life for yourself, but for your children too. Maybe my parents were too selfish to understand this concept. My parents or their parents never thought, "How will this affect my children?" I can't begin to imagine how far back these toxic feelings and behaviors went. And both my parents?! Sheesh.

The same feelings plagued me. Depression. Guilt. An uncertainty about life. Lack of attention. I could have numbed my feelings of abandonment and resentment with drugs and alcohol at any age, but I didn't. There was a huge possibility that once day I would. It was then I realized I didn't want to pass these feelings to my children. I didn't want to allow my grief and anger to have me turn to drugs and alcohol. I didn't want to waddle in the negative feelings that can fuel self-destructive and toxic behavior. I wanted better for the children I knew I wanted and would eventually have.

Black families have a habit of sitting in their dysfunction. They bury family secrets and familial hurt. All the while pretending everything is okay because of fear of judgment and embarrassment all to the detriment of the victim and sometimes themselves. Families never want to admit or discuss that "Big Mamma" outside of providing shelter may have done a horrible job of raising not just her kids, but generations. People would rather sit in familiar pain than take a step into the unknown towards getting help, acknowledging dysfunction and growing. Therapy is taboo in certain communities. Growing up I would always try and hide my parent's drug use. I don't know if it was embarrassment or a fear of possible judgement. After this realization, I knew in order to be a better parent than they were, I had to first forgive them. Then acknowledge that their presence or lack thereof had a profound effect on me. No matter how many stand in's or other resources I had access to, Irving and Alberta were needed and missed.

So, I began the painstaking process of forgiveness. Just so we are clear it wasn't easy or fast. I cried a lot. I cursed a lot and I had to be okay with a lot of unanswered questions, but most of all I talked about it. I was honest in all of my feelings. The strongest being I felt like since they were dead, they were getting off easy. Where is the accountability? So, they just get off scot free?

Forgiveness is hard. It always made me feel like I was being taken advantage of. Like I was conceding a match to a less formidable opponent. Where I grew up, we made fun of losers, so I associated being the forgiving person as the loser. That was my ego making me feel less than. Forgiveness is the removal of the ego. There are no winners or losers. Whew! That's hard writing it, nevertheless doing it. Forgiveness is emotional. Forgiveness is draining. Forgiveness must be an intentional effort to change your feelings. It's a process. You must talk it out.

Therapy consisted of a lot of talking. Talking allowed me to hear myself. I was being open and honest about my feelings of hurt and abandonment instead of keeping them hidden. For years I didn't talk about how I felt about my parents. I would just smile and acknowledge how much I missed them by unearthing the same memories as proof that I cared. I didn't want to seem like a bitter adult that couldn't forgive her parents, but that's who I had become.

Seeing a therapist is something I strongly recommend. You don't always need a tragic event or the loss of a loved one to prompt you to go. It's okay to need help just to cope with the hectic emotions of everyday life. Compounded grief. Grief and trauma don't always mean death. Some people aren't equipped to handle the stressors of jobs while balancing a family and other relationships. Toss in the era of social media and it's a breeding ground for mental instability. Go see a therapist. Talk to someone. Cry and yell at God! It was the best thing I could have done for myself.

Just as one needs tools to build a house, we need tools to help cope and therapy can assist you with obtaining those tools. Don't be afraid to do something for your own mental well-being, even if it means getting professional help.

I realized that in the throes of my grief. What good can I possibly be to my wife or anyone else in this condition? It's one of the reasons I didn't look for a job right away. What can I possibly commit to or bring to any company crying all day? I don't just mean professional, but personal relationships as well. If I wasn't married and knew my wife loved me and would take care of me, I'm not sure I would be able to emotionally contribute to a relationship. We must do a better job of putting mental and emotional health first! If you're not committed to being emotionally stable, then how can you commit to anything or anyone else? Take the mask off. We are not okay every day.

A scab is a dry, rough protective crust that forms over a cut or wound during healing. That's what therapy was for me. A SCAB. I was able to heal in a protective environment. Again, this doesn't mean it was easy by any means. I had to admit to deeply rooted anger and resentment of the past to begin to address the current issues that bothered me. I had to fall apart and allow my therapist to assist me in making myself whole again. It was initially painful, but the sessions became easier over time. Therapists "ASSISTS" us. Ultimately the difficult work is up to us. People would like to believe we saunter into these weekly appointments, lay on some couch for an hour only to sashay out renewed and repaired. Ha! It's hard work. People have no idea how many times I dreaded therapy in order to hide from the work. Find a great therapist that you trust and put in the work. We must talk about our issues. None of this works without being able to honestly communicate your feelings.

Now here I am with an amazing therapist, but I was still struggling a bit. Something didn't feel right physically. I was a bit moody and tired often. So, what did I do? What everyone else does that has questions. I went to Google. *insert blank stare* I tend to "Google" diagnose myself. Don't laugh; we have all done it before. For some reason, even with therapy, my brain wouldn't shut off. In a panic or efforts to second guess our doctors most of us go to the internet seeking answers to medical questions without knowing how much anxiety this can cause.

During one of my late-night web searches I discovered the five stages of grief.

1. Denial/Isolation

2. Anger

3. Bargaining

4. Depression

5. Acceptance

That's it! I jumped up! I'm on the 5 Stage of Grief runaway train. I jumped out of bed and began pacing back and forth. You couldn't tell me I wasn't going through all of them. I kept analyzing myself in anticipation of the next step trying to rush the process. I was confused as to what was taking me so long to get to ACCEPTANCE. I wanted to be done with it already. I thought acceptance would make the pain stop.

I thought my body was aware of these stages and knew at what point to shift my feelings. I would sit in my room for hours reading Diyah's and Kindel's obituaries and looking up my symptoms on Google. I played out the different scenarios of their deaths had I been present. "Yep. This is definitely DENIAL", I thought. I was angry at my uncles and male cousins for not properly vetting Diyah's boyfriend during the last family cookout before her death. Isn't that what uncles and brothers are supposed to do? Ask a million questions with a scowl on your face implying what will happen to you if you hurt our princess. Of course, a concerned uncle putting the fear of God into your boyfriend will prevent him from killing you... NOT.

I was angry with everyone regarding Kindel's death, mainly myself. I was angry at myself for not making the trip. My wife and I were supposed to be there. If I was there this would not have happened, I agonized repeatedly. YES, YES that's me. I'm in the angry phase. I also exhibited signs of depression. I slept all day and evening. I felt a sense of helplessness. I was pretty sure of my "self-diagnosis" and was determined to share my findings with my therapist during our next session. Here I am thinking she's great. How could she have missed this?

Coincidentally, at the same time I was having horrible menstrual cycles that included headaches, vomiting and nausea. I was all messed up. My gynecologist mentioned I had a chemical imbalance and diagnosed me with PMDD (premenstrual dysphoric disorder). He prescribed a drug named Lexapro. My physical pain coupled with my emotional suffering made me take them without question. I didn't do any research at all on the drug. One of the most noticeable symptoms was "extreme mood shifts." If any medicine has a side effect, I'm sure to experience them. It's just my luck. Great, I thought another darn condition. Often the potential side effects of medication have no bearing on our decisions to take them because we want relief so badly. That was me when I was prescribed Lexapro. I practically ran to the pharmacy with the prescription. Finally, my next therapy session and I mentioned to my therapist about the 5 stages of grief.

Here I was trying to tell her how to cure me. She would go on to explain the 5 stages of grief were initially referring to terminally ill patients. Some grieving people experience those traits, but she didn't think I did. I stared at her questioning her judgment for the first time ever. If I wasn't experiencing The Five Stages of Grief, then what was wrong with me? It was so difficult to stop my mind from racing. I think I wanted to have a "condition". Some sort of ailment to explain my feelings. I couldn't understand why it was so hard to be happy most of the time. She calmed me down and assured me it was normal for me to be anxious about my feelings. I was overreacting as usual.

It was then she mentioned I see a Psychiatrist within the practice. She thought maybe I needed some medication. At first, I declined. Not only was there a stigma around black people and depression, I most certainly didn't want to take any medication for it. However, at this point I had nothing to lose. I was willing to try anything. I gave in and went to see the Psychiatrist.

After our first session, he agreed with the therapist that a small dose of an anti-depressant would help me. As we were going over any medications I was taking at the time, I mentioned the Lexapro from my Gynecologist. His face lit up, but I was totally confused. See, I thought, these doctors just want to keep us on drugs. There went my brain again. He went on to explain how Lexapro was used to treat depression as well.

Because of the medication I would be seeing him from now on and not the therapist. Wait? I'm depressed? I sighed deeply, but I gave in, Lexapro it was. I call it my accidental cure. Most people aren't advocates for therapy or medications; they believe prayer cures all things. I don't believe we can pray away the effects of trauma. God gives us the wisdom to know when it's time to seek professional help. If you contracted the flu or another serious illness you would see a doctor. Why don't we have the same diligence regarding our mental health?

After two months on the medication the PMS symptoms improved, but not without some side effects and I was still struggling to be happy. The medicine decreased my libido and made me feel like I was moving in slow motion. If I missed a dose, I would get this horrible headache. I guess it was leveling out any chemical imbalances I was told I had, but also, I was becoming dependent on medication. I never got used to needing medication in order to help me function. This is when I learned happiness is a choice. I was choosing to be sad and not trying to train my brain to be happy. There was no happy switch, but there is effort. I had to make the effort in order to feel better. The pills couldn't do it alone.

I felt like a zombie. The physical pain was slowly subsiding but at what cost. I didn't feel like myself anymore. I didn't like the idea of "needing" medication. I felt like I had to pop a pill to be normal and I didn't like it one bit. Months passed and after a while I didn't recognize myself. I was a cardboard cutout of my former self, propped up by a prescription. I was faking it to make it. I pretended everything was okay. I hid my depression very well. I didn't even tell my family I was on medication. I figured if I became too withdrawn, they would notice. So, I became funny. I made jokes all the time. I was funny as hell; however, I was dying inside.

Months of therapy and Lexapro slowly turned into a year. I often felt like a dark cloud was following me around like on the cartoons and whenever I would feel better it would rain on my head. I wanted my smile back again. Not to mention my sex drive. I remember thinking this sad stuff is a bummer. If only it was as easy as "willing" myself to feel better. My little pep talks I would have with myself in the mirror were of no help. I felt like I was at rock bottom. I had hit the floor. No faith. No job. My heart was broken and so was my spirit. I was exasperated. I felt like I was swimming against the current and couldn't do it anymore.

I felt like Jim Carey in Bruce Almighty in the scene when he yells, "Smite me oh mighty Smiter." The thing about being at your lowest point is, well… it's the LOWEST POINT. I promise you can't fall off the floor.

You must determine how long you're going to stay down there. Once I realized I was at rock bottom I decided to use it as my foundation. At the bottom is where I began to slowly gather the tools I needed to put myself back together again.

A change of heart was my starting point. Once you change your heart your actions will change as well. I resigned to the fact that in putting the pieces back together I may not be the same, but I would be whole again. A different you is better than a broken you, so it's okay if some people say you've changed. Some life experiences force us to change. It's detrimental to our emotional stability to evolve.

More than physically I felt my spirit yearning for healing. It's like something clicked inside of me and I wanted to live! I wanted off the meds. I wanted my smile back and darn it I was going to get it. It's okay not to be okay. Everyone doesn't have it all together. People just pretend very well.

"The only cure for grief is action."

—George Henry Lewes [4]

Exercise is where I started. I noticed I would feel better if I moved around more. I began to walk a lot and doing anything to move my limbs, especially on sunny days. Every morning I would whisper to myself, "Get up girl," over and over until I moved. My neighbors didn't understand why I would park the car down the block when we had a garage. It was so I had a longer walk to my house. I would take long walks in the park, preferably one with a lake. It was the first time in a long time that I welcomed the water view and wasn't cursing God. Some days I listened to music as I walked and some days I listened to the sounds of the streets. It didn't matter whether it was horns honking or the loud revving of engines from busses and trucks or the wind whipping past my face on cold days. I was tuned in! I would look around and see people walking in their own little world which made me realize how small I had assumed the world to be. Well at least my views anyways. I glanced at people behind the wheels of the vehicles and wondered where everyone was off to in what seemed like such a rush. Were they late, were their gas tanks full? I did everything to keep my mind working and from turning to mush.

One of my favorite places to walk to was the library. It was always quiet and although I enjoyed the sounds of the streets the solitude of the book stacks was always a welcome respite. I read everything I could get my hands on. I read magazines, newspapers, books, billboards, labels on products, and my favorite since I was a kid the back of the cereal box. During my reading I discovered Echart Tolle, Marian Williamson, Tony Robbins, and Deepak Chopra to name a few.

In October 2009 Oprah Winfrey interviewed Jay-Z for O Magazine. In case you didn't know Jay-Z is my favorite rapper and I was very excited when I saw him standing there, next to Oprah Winfrey, outside of the Marcy Housing Projects in the heart of Brooklyn. Oprah was like the Holy Trinity of Journalism. If she ever found you interesting and was lucky enough to get an interview it was an indication you had "made it." It was right before his 40th birthday and he discussed how he first started out selling records from the trunk of his car to reconciling with his dad. It was a great interview, but what stuck out for me was in closing out the article Jay-Z told Oprah about the five books that had the most influence on his life. Jay-z talked about forgiving his dad and therapy that helped him be a better person. I figured some answers had to be in these books that he recommended. The Seat of the Soul by Gary Zukav, The Celestine Prophecy by James Redfield, The Purple Cow by Seth Godin, The Odyssey by Homer, and Outliers by Malcolm Gladwell.

If these helped to change Jay-z' life, then what would the harm be in me reading them? I thought. I checked the library but they didn't have any of the books. I didn't let that stop me though. I practically ran home, hopped in the car and hurried over to the nearest Barnes and Noble. The first two I purchased was The Seat of the Soul and The Celestine Prophecy. I hadn't felt good in a long time, but I felt good leaving Barnes and Noble that day. After reading the books I felt a jolt of energy go through me. This was an unfamiliar feeling. I felt a surge of light in my spirit that I hadn't felt in a long time.

I walked daily, I read, and I talked about my feelings in therapy. My therapist helped me remove the burden of guilt, by helping me understand none of these deaths were not my fault. There was nothing I could have done to change the outcome. Becoming what

I perceived to be a better daughter still would not have changed my parents' lifestyle. It also didn't mean they didn't love me. It just means they weren't capable. Seth was determined to kill Nadiyah whether it was December 8th or December 10th. No matter if I was there or not. He wanted her dead. There was no way I could have saved her. It's okay to cry and mourn and be angry. Just don't get stuck in the emotions. Feel them and allow them to move through you. Don't allow your emotions to clog your heart. Your heart's main job is to pump blood to and from your body. If it gets backed up and overrun with emotions you can have an anxiety attack or literally die from a broken heart. Let the emotions flow.

"He who learns must suffer. And even in our sleep pain that cannot forget falls drop by drop upon the heart, and in our own despair, against our will, comes wisdom to us by the awful grace of God."

—Aeschylus [5]

CHAPTER 6

Grace

There is always an event that leads us to big "aha" moments in our lives. For me it was the moment I forgave my cousin's murderer. Two years after Nadiyah's death my wife and I were going through a rough time in our marriage. I'm not sure if it was finances or my incessant need for attention during my grieving. I was unfaithful in my marriage and didn't want to deal with the recourse. I was having a tantrum. Rather than constantly hurting each other deliberately, we decided to separate for a while. Throughout everything we have been through, love has always been the glue to our bond. I never stopped loving my wife. No matter what else I got involved in.

I came back to New Jersey and she was still in Virginia. I kept up my financial responsibilities to our home thinking it would somehow make me less of a villain. I remember calling her about our dog and she didn't answer. She always answered for me. I called her mom and some mutual friends. Still nothing. After donning my detective hat, I found out she was on a date. My ego had me furious. It had to be my ego, because I was sleeping with someone else. Why the heck should I care what she was doing? Because she was Mrs. Callender. She was my wife. As I hung up the phone, I felt my flesh became extremely hot and I began to pace the floor. Back and forth, back and forth. I was starting to make myself dizzy. What was this feeling? I felt a surge go through my extremities. It felt like my body was overheating and within minutes all I saw was red.

Before I knew it, I was getting dressed and looking for my car keys. As I'm rummaging through the house looking for my keys a sinister plan was unfolding in my mind. It's like there were two people up there. The angry jealous person was looking for the keys to drive six hours to Virginia Beach purchase a gun at Walmart and blow her brains out. Yep, that's what I'm going to do. I'm going to kill her. It was the moment I said this out loud that I stopped. Not only had I spotted the keys but another little voice inside of me said you're going to do what?! That's the plan? The other voice said, "Hell yea!" I grabbed the keys and made it to the front door, when suddenly my feet became stuck. There was a mirror by the front door on the way out. I looked at myself and there he was. Seth. I was Seth going to kill Nadiyah. In that instance images of me sitting in church as a kid began to flash in my head. I felt an overwhelming sense of God's presence in the room. Distinguishing between God's voice and your ego takes discernment.

I dropped to the floor and immediately began praying. I was rocking back and forth crying uncontrollably and praying. I kept asking God to remove the anger. Remove the hurt. Remove the jealousy. Remove whatever feeling that was pushing me to WANT to get into my car and drive to Virginia and kill Kayla. I knew enough to call on God for strength and guidance even though we hadn't spoken in so long he showed up for me. THAT'S GRACE! I didn't deserve it, but he saved me. Most people don't have that. Most people don't know to call on God in their darkest hours. Even though we hadn't spoken in a while I did. I stayed on that floor in front of the door for hours, just crying, calling on God for help and releasing pain.

This pain wasn't even about my wife and I anymore. It was the pain and agony of my cousin's death finally exiting my body. It was me understanding that not everyone hears that little voice or feels God's presence. Everyone doesn't have the inclination to call on a higher power to thwart them from committing a heinous act. Seth didn't know enough to call on God. He didn't know. He couldn't have.

Favor ain't fair!! I used to hear people use that expression all the time. This doesn't mean I received a blessing that you or anyone else wasn't worthy of, nor is it because God loves me more than anyone else. It simply means I received a blessing even though I didn't deserve it. Despite whom I am or what I did, or what I was thinking of doing; God saved me. THAT'S GRACE!! I was so angry with God. I blamed him for everything yet needed him to fix it. I was too hurt and angry to ask for help, but he helped me anyway. That's GRACE. He loved me in-spite of my anger. He kept blessing me even when I wasn't talking to him. He kept me from ruining my life. A bunch of people's lives.

He kept me from becoming what hurt me so much. That is Grace! Grace is not something we have to bargain for or trade off. There's no test to pass in order to receive grace. God's Grace is not Couture. It doesn't come in a particular size nor is it seasonal. It's like rain!! It falls upon everyone.

Anger takes up more space in your heart than love. It's so much easier to be angry at someone than to love or forgive them. Forgiveness isn't the easiest thing to do. Especially if you see the person often and their presence brings up hurt or resentment. However, the hardest thing in the world to do is forgive yourself. Not forgiving yourself opens the door for you to question everything you thought you knew and loved about yourself. It turns into self-sabotaging. Forgiveness isn't a familiar feeling that's why many people don't practice forgiveness. Why should I exert so much effort into forgiving someone that has caused me so much pain? Then it hit me. Duh! Because God forgave you when you ask it of him. You cannot ask for God's Grace and not extend it to someone else.

I was introduced to God at an early age. No, wait let me rephrase that. I was introduced to Church at an early age. However, as I grew older, I realized the Bible as it was being read to me was boring. It had amazing stories but was very boring and I always struggled to understand what was being told to me. Once I realized I could connect with God outside of the actual church structure, things became better for me. I had to get to know God for myself and on my own terms. I kept expecting the God my grandmother introduced to me to show up. Remember I spoke about the white, straight-haired guy that rides in on the clouds? Yeah! I was waiting for that guy! I had an idea of what our encounter should be and when it didn't happen that way, I lost faith. What bothered me about organized religion was the politics involved. I noticed Churches had cliques that reminded me of the high school days. It was tiring. The God of my understanding didn't' have favorites nor was he confined to a "building". He ended up being wherever I needed him be. I discovered that spirituality for me was the need to connect to a higher power outside of what I've heard preached by various Pastors. Don't get me wrong. I've heard a great word of God preached over my lifetime. It just wasn't enough for me.

A light bulb had clicked on in my heart and spirit. I decided to go back to God myself and learn about what other "religions" thought and believed him to be to them. I wanted to feel him outside of the bible stories. I wanted God off those pages so to speak. So, I stopped the monotone prayers. I prayed everywhere all the time. I read self-help books and meditated. I sincerely asked the creator to make me whole again, because the glue these people were using wasn't holding.

The meds were the glue!! I prayed for strength. I prayed for clarity. I prayed for peace. I'm going to keep saying forgiveness is the key! I prayed for the ability to forgive. I asked him to show up differently for me. Forgiving my parents for choices they weren't equipped to make was difficult but became easier once I recognized they just didn't have the tools to be whom I needed them to be. You can't be angry at someone for building a raggedy house and not putting mortar between the bricks. There's a big difference in not having mortar and not knowing you're supposed to use mortar in the first place. Some people's foundations don't have mortar because they're being cheap and trying to use shortcuts. It's the people that didn't even know to use mortar; those were my parents. The ones without the proper tools.

During this process I learned that God is the ultimate fixer and not me. It's at your darkest moments when he shows up. He humbled me tremendously. I had to realize he does things on his time and not ours. Here I was cursing him and I just wasn't ready.

Your plan may not be God's plan. He keeps us in situations for his purposes. We must build up our faith so that no matter how bad things are you believe God for his sovereignty. There is power in your process. God uses your pain as an example to someone else that they too can make it. Don't be ashamed of what you go through. Stand in your truth. If standing in your truth makes anyone else uncomfortable then they have a problem with their own story.

"The ultimate measure of a person is not where
they stand in 'moments of convenience,' but
where they stand in 'moments of challenge,'
moments of great crisis and controversy."

—Martin Luther King [6]

Chapter 7

Gratitude

A fter Grace rains down on you, Gratitude is like the sunshine after the rain. You need gratitude to keep the flowers in constant bloom - to feel great. Once God healed my broken heart, I was so grateful. Little things out of place in my life didn't have such a negative impact on me anymore because of my gratitude. For me to constantly be grateful, I had to rid myself of the heavy emotional things that weighed me down which in turn opened my heart up to gratitude. According to Merriam Webster's definition, Gratitude is a noun that means the quality of being thankful. Readiness to show appreciation for and to return kindness. Arrogance, ego, and insecurity are so heavy. They prevented me from being grateful. I begin to fill myself with lighter things like humility, service, meditation and scriptures. Humility is lighter than arrogance. The ego weighs you down like a bag of rocks. Can you imagine how slow and sluggish one has to be with a bag of rocks on their back. Odell Beckham Jr would never be where the quarterback needed him to be to catch a pass with a bag of rocks slowing him down. That was me dragging around my ego. I was missing everything God had for me, because I was never there at the right time. I found that I was able to unload these things through fasting and mediating. This helped me release whatever that didn't benefit me emotionally or spiritually and in turn I became extremely grateful.

I am even grateful for the bad times. Displaying gratitude sharpens character. The difficult times reminded me that I was alive and to appreciate the good even more. Gratitude and humility helped me to be a better person which in turn would make me a better parent.

I'm in such a happy space some days I pinch myself. I stop and literally listen for the other shoe to drop. There's no other shoe. I used to laugh at people and their daily affirmations and quirky, you go girl moments. Truth be told, it's all needed to keep you going. We must surround ourselves with positivity all the time. Not just people either. I'm talking books, music, movies, and the whole nine yards. For my 40th birthday I had a Book and Brunch. I requested forty books that were all about spirituality and self-help. That was the best decision of my life.

When the negativity or melancholy creeps in I am properly equipped to handle it. I created a happy place and feel good memories that I can retreat to emotionally in case of emergencies. Recognizing triggers keeps you better prepared to push through. If you want to you can do anything! But you must want to. The human spirit is amazingly resilient. Tap into your resiliency. The greatest triumphs in our lives sometimes occur when the circumstances seem to be hardest. Today I'm grateful for my hard times and the lessons. I'm grateful I rekindled my love with God.

We must give God the glory in every situation. I'm grateful that Seth didn't kill the kids. Grateful I had to plan one funeral instead of three. Be at peace with your journey. I'm grateful I worked past so many issues to become a parent and break generational curses. My heart is overflowing with gratitude. Everything is a test of faith. So many voices will say, "You can't do this," - the loudest being your own. Nobody can doubt you and second guess you more than yourself. The key is to be louder! Be louder with your prayer! Be louder with your praise. Be louder with your gratitude.

"You have to find the part of
you that died with her."

—Kayla Callender

Chapter 8

Sugar In My Grits

I've learned some great lessons throughout this entire journey that has brought me from my old broken self to the amazing woman I am meant to be. Trials are necessary to get us to our purpose. You can't build a life on hurt from the past. There must be lessons learned and passed on to help others heal. Here are the best things that I've learned.

1. Heal

Mountains were meant to climb not carry. Release your burdens. We don't need to constantly carry around our hurt and trauma. The misconception about journeys is that there's an end point. If there is a higher level to reach or a goal to achieve it's safe to say the journey isn't over. While on the journey to healing, don't allow a mountain you've carried to leave a chip on your shoulder. Drop that boulder. Where is the lesson if you are bitter? It's okay to put the mountain down and look back at it and say, "I used to be there, but I have worked through that and it doesn't serve my good anymore." Let go of whatever doesn't serve you emotionally or spiritually. Forgive yourself for whatever you couldn't do or thought you should have done. You can heal and be happy. Don't feel guilty about having joy in the end. Understanding that you deserve happiness is one of the key factors to navigating and ultimately conquering the sadness of grief and depression. Healing equals joy.

In order to heal from trauma we must talk about it. Talking about it revisits the pain opening old wounds, hence people not healing properly. No one wants to go through that, however facing your fears will free you from the pain. The longer you take to treat a wound the longer it will take to heal. We can't allow trauma to fester. It will rot your soul, altering your outlook on everything until it ultimately changes who you were meant to be. Unhealed, we unknowingly pass the trauma, grief, and depression to our children.

Whether it's how we treat them, our behavior, or how we treat others, creating generational curses. Children are always watching their parents or caretakers. It's who they look to for guidance and understanding of this world. So, if you're a damaged person imagine all the harm you can do. Grief isn't only about mourning for dead things. It's also about mourning the unexpected loss of anything you may have loved. A failed romantic relationship, a job, or even severed friendships that we thought would last forever. The first love of my life broke my heart. It wasn't intentional, but my heart didn't understand intention, only the pain that followed. The course of my entire life changed because I didn't grieve the loss of my first love. I moved on too soon in order to prevent from feeling the pain. I didn't allow myself time to heal so the next relationship was spent searching for what I was missing ignoring the fact I wasn't even in love with the guy.

I thought I was. Truthfully, he just filled a void. Never fill voids. Find your peace and heal.

What is it that you need to let go that's preventing you from healing? What and whom do you need to grieve for? Living or deceased

_____

_____

_____

_____

_____

_____

_____

_____

_____

_____

_____

_____

2. SPIRITUALITY

God doesn't live in church. He will show up when you need him the most, wherever you need him to be. What you think is your breaking point may very well be your breakthrough. HOLD ON. Fear is a real thing, but prayer is stronger. Spirituality transcends religion. Don't allow people to project their beliefs and interpretation of doctrine on to you. Don't let church hurt keep you from loving a higher power. Find out who God is for yourself. He is something different to and for all of us. Just like your natural parents, God teaches us lessons that don't always feel good. It doesn't mean that he doesn't love you or that he has forgotten you. Form a relationship with him and stay in constant communication. YOUR WAY. I didn't start to feel a connection with God and the universe until I stopped using other people's prayers. I'm not telling people to not attend church, or to not trust the clergy. That's not my message here. I'm a member of a church and the fellowship and relationships keep me grounded. Me and God have our own thang going on. Get your own thing going on with a higher power, any higher power you choose. Find something to believe in. Something that makes you want to be a better person. Something that makes you want to change the world. Something that gives you faith! I choose God.

I was an unemployed cheater and God saved me. When your life is a mess, he will take you from selfishness to service. I was going to the beach every day complaining about my life, but clearly missing the wonder of the sunrise and sunsets. I absolutely feel like I've lost a lot, but I've been saved from so much more. No one can replace the lives lost or the longing for them, but you can find renewed purpose in life through spirituality.

The hardest thing in the world is to be angry with God and still trust him. You may not agree with his plans, but you do have to trust him. Faith is blind. It's about trusting when you cannot see a way or understand the reasons. We must stop trying to figure out God. If we could figure him out totally then he wouldn't be God. Fall into him. Lean on him. Lean into him and stay faithful. I promise he won't let you down.

What gives you faith and hope? Are you living by example? What can you do better? What are ways do you need to stop doubting your faith?

_____

_____

_____

_____

_____

_____

_____

_____

_____

_____

3. Legacy Over Lineage

I learned that from my cousin Os. My parents are my lineage, not my legacy. I create my own Legacy. Life is about choices. I was broken by my parents' choices, but I chose to fix myself. I choose to be better because I knew I wanted kids one day. Make better choices. All choices aren't easy.12I want to be remembered for my choices, not the choices my parents made.

   Most of all I don't want to spend my life blaming them for my emotional short comings, so I made the choice to forgive them. There's no greater gift you can give your family and children than being present for them. People will always remember how you made them feel and not what you gave them. Acceptance doesn't mean resignation. You can accept what happened to you, but you don't have to resign to fact that it's who you are. It's what creates generational curses and allows them to seep down into other generations. It stops with me! At least for my son. He will not have to hide behind any of my shames or the sins of his grandparents and great grandparents. There's this awful unspoken rule within black families, "What happens in this house stays in the house." It's stupid and unhealthy. It's a cowardly way to cover up the wrong doings within the family dynamic with embarrassment and threats of not being accepted by the family anymore. Don't keep silent and risk your sanity because of someone else's sins. Your sanity and peace of mind is more important than someone else's pride, ego and lack of humility. Broken familial relationships is like a floor with tiny broken pieces of glass everywhere. If you do not properly pick up the pieces someone else comes along, i.e younger generations, steps on the broken glass and gets hurt as well. Clean up your family's broken glass and save the other generations some pain. Break Generational Curses.

Healthy trees can't grow from rotten roots. Remove your damaged tree to healthy soil for your kids. The old rotten roots may be your lineage, but it doesn't have to be your legacy. It's not about your trials, but how you handle them that creates your legacy. We can't control tragedies nor our past, but we can control how we react and adapt to them.

What are negative ties that make you feel bonded in shame to family? What negative traits do you think were passed to you that you would like to let go of?

_____

_____

_____

_____

_____

_____

_____

_____

_____

_____

_____

4. MEDITATION

Meditating isn't about feeling good, it's about being mindful. Acknowledge your breaths and allow them to slow enough that you can feel your heartbeat. It's about being still. It helps you reboot; like a pacemaker or defibrillator does to your heart. Try it out for at least 15 minutes any time of the day - ANYWHERE. Being mindful decreases bad decisions that can be made in the heat of the moment and decreases anxiety. The time it takes to refocus and take a couple of breaths can lead to positive outcomes that panic and nervousness normally have control over. If you can't get to a quiet place use a mantra to drown out the sounds. If you can't feel your heartbeat you can hear your own voice. Mediation allows you to harness and exhale the sad feelings. It lets you know you're still alive. Meditation doesn't bring you peace, it helps you stop disturbing what's already there.

Our peace lies within us. We just need to tap into it. Oftentimes we have so much going on we are led to believe we have to go looking for what lies within. Most times the quietness will lead me to pray and talk to God. It's when things are most quiet, I can hear his voice. I search for him to soothe me during mediation. Sometimes he doesn't respond but bestows enough peace upon me to quietly drift off into a light sleep. Briefly going to a place untouched by earthly worry and strife. It doesn't come easy either. Worry and angst will slip into your thoughts when you are trying to be still. The key is to stay focused and keep pushing out negative thoughts with stillness and prayer. Your mind doesn't know what to do with silence on its own. You must train it.

Meditation restores my soul. There are days when I'm dealing with so much and if I don't get a quiet place to breath it out it builds up. Only to come crashing down around me days later in the form a mini crying breakdown. I guess it's a preventative measure in a sense.

Why aren't you making time for stillness? Spend one hour a day intentionally making time to be still. Clear your mind and acknowledge your breaths. The noise will not stop right away but give it a few days. Come back after 30 days and write what feels different?

_____

_____

_____

_____

_____

_____

_____

_____

_____

_____

5. Likes Doesn't Translate To Love

We must stop letting social media run our life. This didn't start with Facebook and Instagram or Twitter. This goes back to Myspace. I had a Myspace page. I was friends with Tom. Who wasn't? LOL. I transitioned to Facebook in November 2008 right before Nadiyah's murder. When my Facebook memories from that time come across my timeline I look back and cringe. I was unraveling right before my "friends" eyes. I didn't know Facebook wasn't the place to have an obvious minor breakdown. I was being myself. I was being honest in my feelings with people that I thought were my friends and cared about me. Looking back, I'm not sure what I was expecting from everyone. People are rarely themselves on social media. I consider myself one of the few people that are honest in these forums. It can become overwhelming sharing so much with people waiting and expecting them to like, love, or comment on your picture or post that you spent hours trying to perfect.

The number of friends or people that follow you isn't an indication of who you are as a person. It doesn't make you any more or less important to people that genuinely love you. Friends do more than click like or love on a social media post. They pick up the phone to hear your voice. When you don't pick up the phone, they drive to your house to check on you. Take frequent social media breaks. Social media takes away from personal relationships. It makes people more distant. People start to hide behind the keyboard and the isolation negatively affects your health. Stop living your life in a fishbowl. We can't keep secretly comparing our life to others on these social media platforms. It allows people to pretend they have it all together all the time when they really don't. This makes others reluctant to share their difficult times. What happens when you're really going through something? People don't care much while you're down in a real low place. GET OUT AND THEN TELL ME ABOUT IT, is sadly our culture. People don't want to hear your woes while you're down and out. They don't give two cents about your trials and hard times. They don't care about your valley story! Only your glory.

Take a social media break. Delete the apps if necessary. It's okay I must delete mine from time to time. Fill that time with other things. What other ways did you communicate with people during the break? What did you do in place of uploading your social media?

_____

_____

_____

_____

_____

_____

_____

_____

_____

_____

_____

6. LAUGH

Laughing during grief is like physical therapy after an injury. It works your muscles. Each night may feel like the end of the world but opening your eyes the next morning is proof that it's not. "Weeping may last through the night, but joy comes in the morning," Psalm 30:5. Keep looking forward to the morning. Watch funny movies. Laugh at yourself! You must constantly work to stay happy. Smile for no reason. Even today I find myself frowning for no reason. I must stop whatever I'm doing and remind myself I'm okay. Everything is good. When laughing the brain also releases endorphins that can relieve some physical pain. Smile and always believe something good is about to happen. Don't allow people to project their issues on to you. It's okay to allow a friend to vent without inheriting their issues. Say good morning to strangers more often. We don't know what people are dealing with. You never know what will make someone's day.

What's so funny? I used to be afraid to laugh with my mother. Whenever she couldn't get high nothing was funny, so I never knew when to laugh. When I say afraid, I don't mean a fear of being beaten. I mean the fear of her look of anger, disappointment and sadness. That fear stole my laugh. Don't let life steal your laugh.

What are you laughing at? What makes you smile? What have you done today to make someone else laugh or smile?

_____

_____

_____

_____

_____

_____

_____

_____

_____

_____

_____

7. Grief Has No Cure

Death doesn't mean the absence of God. Imagining life without our loved ones gives us anxiety and invokes panic as we often wonder what we will do without them. There is no magic pill you can take to feel better. Be patient with yourself. I don't think we ever stop grieving we just find better coping mechanisms. GO TO THERAPY! Discover a hobby. Do something you like every day. The tricky thing with grief is we start to associate it with death only. There are relationships we have with people that are alive that aren't healthy that we need to let go and mourn them. GO TO THERAPY! There are relationships we need to let go for our own sanity, spiritual growth, and emotional stability. Stop staying in toxic relationships even if it's your parents or siblings. Loyalty should not come at the expense of your sound mind. And it's okay not to get closure. I know it sucks, but we can do more emotional damage searching for a "why" from a person that can't give it. Most times people don't know their own why, let alone to be able to provide you with one. I did say to go therapy, right?

Stop expecting an ending point and just ride the wave. Nadiyah has been dead for 11 years at the time of this writing. Most days are great, then there are times when I find myself picking up the phone to call her. Next thing I know I'm balling, crying my eyes out. Here comes a wave. I look at my son and see Kindel. Some days I smile and other times tears well up in my eyes. Here comes the wave. The idea is not to try and prevent the wave, but to recognize it's coming and ride it out. Surf baby!!

Firsts are the worst! The first everything you have to experience without your loved one is the hardest thing to endure. Don't let "what if's" waste the gift of the present. Don't let traditions die with our loved ones. Keeping their memory alive will make you smile more. Grief is more than sadness. It's the pieces of your broken heart floating in the stillness of your chest cavity bumping into other organs as it searches for a regular rhythm again. Colliding when memories arise. Grief is internally painful. Silence is a two faced. It can be of help or hinderance. Use the daunting silence to collect your thoughts and remember the happy times, never allowing it to bully you into loneliness.

It's a never-ending journey missing loved ones. Travel light because it's a heck of a ride.

Have you acknowledged your grief today? If not, Why? What helped you move through the feelings? What seems to be keeping you stuck? Is the silence a help or hinderance? Why?

_____

_____

_____

_____

_____

_____

_____

_____

_____

_____

8. Mommy/Daddy Issues

Whether we love them or hate them, your parent's presence or absence influences who you become. A girl's father should always be her first love. He will set the stage for what she ultimately expects from a mate. Security, love and protection. Have you ever noticed a woman's face during the father daughter dance at her wedding? After staring lovingly into his eyes, her head comes to rest on his shoulder, where she will smile slightly, then exhale. If no standards are set by daddy women develop "daddy issues". Stop making "daddy issue decisions." This applies to men and women!! If your father is dead or you guys are just in a space whereas conveying your feelings won't help..., write a letter and burn it. Release that energy. My therapist had me write letters to my father expressing my hurt, anger and overall disappointments in his decisions. Initially I thought it was so silly pouring out my heart and laying my feelings bare on pages to a person that would never see it, nevertheless understand.

It's your mind's job to protect the heart. Once I stopped overthinking it, I ended up with pages of emotions that I had no idea where inside of me. You can't allow the negative feelings to affect your judgement. Some of us are functioning in pain bodies and we don't even know it. We pick our mates and develop personality traits according to our parents. Don't become the person you hate or end up marrying the wrong spouse looking for the daddy you never had or felt was missing. No matter how much Big Dad loved and nurtured me, I still missed my father Irving as I got older. I wondered about his favorite color, football team, and what foods he did or didn't like. Therapy, time, and becoming a parent has turned my resentment into hope. Hope that if my parents were still alive, they would have turned their lives around to be more present.

Fathers, Grandfathers, Godfathers, men in general, are a very vital part of who we become. None of the above in your life get a mentor. A good one. Find one for your kid. Go to therapy so you can identify those negative feelings that you're projecting and possibly stunting your emotional growth. Therapy doesn't always have to be for grief or sadness. Not everyone can handle life's disappointments and unexpected twists and turns. It's okay to need therapy for things besides grief.

If your parents are deceased is there something you never got tell them? If they are alive and your relationship is estranged is there something you want to say to them? Has the relationship with your parents or lack thereof affected you in a positive way or negative way? If you are married or in a relationship, do you believe you chose your spouse because of parental qualities the possessed? Why or why not?

_____

_____

_____

_____

_____

_____

_____

_____

_____

_____

9. FASTING/DIET

You are what you eat has never made sense to me until now. It's so easy to get lost in a tub of ice cream and chocolate chip cookies when you're sad. After a month, you look up and notice the double chin and your clothes are too tight. We must be conscience of emotional eating. The fact that we believe food is comforting has to do with controlling our thoughts and ideas about food. Removing food intermittently gave me spiritual clarity. Once my mind was not on how many Oreos I could eat I was forced to focus on other things. Fasting helped me do this.

Fasting is not about starving yourself in order to get God's attention. It's about seeking a more intimate relationship with him. Fasting is about raising your level of spirituality. Medication helped me manage grief and depression, but it was my faith that eventually pulled me through. When you come to a space in life where you can't hear God anymore, it means things are too hectic. Hectic doesn't always mean a bad thing. For example, you may be offered what you have perceived to be a great career opportunity. Instead of fasting, humbly going to God in prayer, and waiting to hear from him we make these snap decisions on our own. T may not be immediately, it may take several years before it comes to pass that it was not for you.

The first time I couldn't hear God anymore was during my period of grief. It was so quiet I got scared. I used to be able to talk to him a lot, however when I went to him about my cousin and nephew's death, I couldn't hear him. Although I was looking for a "why" I would have taken anything. I just wanted to hear his voice and when I didn't it made me overwhelmingly sad. I'm crying writing this because I vividly remember the darkness and pain associated with the silence.

The disappointment and agony of assuming he abandoned me in my most desolate time confused me.

I thought he was angry with me. Back then I didn't know that Fasting was how you prepare your body and mind to have deeper conversations with him. It clears your mind beyond belief. Sure, I hear from God in my prayers. I also talk to him while I am on a ladder fixing an operating room light, while stuck in traffic, or sitting in a sports bar watching a game. I remember once I went to watch a football game alone and someone asked if they could sit next to me. I told them someone was sitting there just so they wouldn't overhear mine and God's conversation. I told you all he does not live in church.

My church introduced me to Fasting in January 2015. It was the Daniel Fast. I thought I would die without bacon, root beer, and sweets. Daniel fasted for three weeks, but our church did the entire month of January. Armed with a list of foods I could and could not eat, a prayer line that we called three times a day I dived in. The prior month my wife and I went to a specialist for a consultation to begin the process of having our baby. "You're overweight, over 40, and African American," the doctor said. She basically dashed all my hopes of fulfilling my lifelong dream.

I said with no hesitation, "That's up to God, if it's his will we shall have a baby." She looked so confused. It appeared she thought her professional opinion would override my faith. I didn't.

By mid-January, the sugar withdrawal headaches stopped, and I learned to cook a few compliant meals. I stopped listening to hip hop radio stations, started walking in the evenings and talking to GOD.

I prayed often and I was feeling great. Did God answer my prayers? Our son is four years old now. No way was it easy and I didn't get pregnant on the first try, but I trusted God. FAST Cleanse your body. The Daniel Fast and intermittent fasting throughout the year keeps me humble. The more you stay humble, the more you keep arrogance and ego away. Arrogance and ego are what makes you think you can beat the sad feelings. Arrogance and ego prevent you from knowing when to get help. I did say GO TO THERAPY, right?

What you eat is directly proportional to how you feel. Humility is lighter than ego.

Check your relationship with your food, it's directly proportional to the hormones in your body. I was able to correct my hormonal imbalance by changing my diet, then in turn slowly getting off the medication. Eat foods that make you feel light and gives you energy. Not only will you feel better physically you will start to heal emotionally. Feeling better about yourself in the process.

What are some bad eating habits you need to let go of? Water, Water, Water. Have you consumed 8 glasses of water today? What unhealthy eating and drinking habits have you developed since grieving? What good or bad eating and drinking habits have you picked up because it keeps the memory of your loved one alive? What other ways can you remember them besides unhealthy eating or drinking?

_____

_____

_____

_____

_____

_____

_____

_____

_____

_____

10. LOVE

Go where love is and always give love. It's so hard to give love when you are in pain. Giving love in turn made me feel better. Love is warm and inviting not judgmental and condescending. Find your tribe. You will need someone to pull you out of the valley, because we can't always make it out alone. Love who you are, and people will love you in return. This doesn't always mean family. I've met and kept some of the best friends by being my authentic self. Allow people to help you. You cannot heal alone.

Plot twist... maybe you aren't grieving but have a loved one or friend that is. What can you do? You can't "cheer" them up. You must constantly reassure them often that you are there if they choose to talk. Friendships require the same amount of love and communication as romantic relationships. Reaffirm your love for them, offer words of comfort, or my favorite... QUIET. The best thing one of my close friends did was come over and hang out and say nothing at all. I knew she was here if I wanted to say anything, but I didn't. We sat on my porch sipping wine and watching the cars go by in silence. Love is an action word. Show up for your friends in pain even if they claim to be okay or don't answer. Check on them. Love on them. Love like there is no tomorrow, because grief will have you to believe it doesn't exist.

I believe hugs have healing power. A person's arms have the power to lovingly hold you together when you are falling apart.

SUGAR IN MY GRITS

What's your favorite song? The one that you stop whatever you're doing and proceed to sing your heart out. The one that make you smile no matter what? And when you do smile what happy memory comes to your mind? What's your favorite place? Have you hung out with loving friends lately? If no why? What's the movie that you absolutely love? How do you know when you're in love?

_____

_____

_____

_____

_____

_____

_____

_____

_____

_____

Do the right thing, not what's expected. You're still here for a reason. Share your lessons. Someone could be doing something to change the world instead of repeating your mistakes. It's okay to disagree, but it must be respectfully. Everyone will not see your point of view. If we all agreed there would be no purple. I've been stretched beyond my imagination, yet I can't think of one-time God has let me down. He may not have shown up when I expected him to, but he's always been there. The edge is scary especially when going back isn't an option. The fear of falling is greater than the idea of soaring. Falling and failure isn't a bad thing. It means you tried. It means you believed enough in yourself to leap. People prefer to be stagnant and complain that shut up and stretch. God doesn't save you so you can go back to be the same person. He scrapes you off the floor for you to live your purpose! He scrapes you off the floor to be an inspiration for someone else struggling to get up! Keep going. Change the plan if necessary.

Find your passion. Set your intentions. Share your gifts and be of service. Live free and sprinkle sugar in your grits if you want to!

Epilogue

Tragedies will happen and the reasons are beyond our control. We can control our reaction to them. We must allow ourselves time to fall apart, grieve and heal. You aren't supposed to pity me and my tragedies but be inspired by my triumphs. My story is encouragement for those that don't see a way out of the darkness. The train doesn't stay in that dark tunnel forever, it merely passes through. There's light at the end of the tunnel. The clouds won't always cover the sky with the heaviness of defeat. The sun rises and will shine on your face again. My life hasn't turned into a fairytale. My story doesn't end with me being an amazing parent, great spouse and superhuman being. It continues with my struggles in parenting, my never-ending work as a wife, and constantly trying to maintain my spiritual footing in this world of imperfections. It's hard. However, I do it with a renewed sense of purpose.

Everything I do is to make sure my son knows I love him and that he will be okay. Why didn't my parents do that for me? I still don't have the answers, but my journey has brought me peace. I'm grateful I was able to work through it. Some days I smile knowing they are proud of me and other days I cry for the same reason. Thank God for my grandma. I say Good Morning sunshine to my family and friends I speak to daily, never missing chances to say, 'I love you.' Simply because Nadiyah said it to me daily and it made my day better. I am living life to the fullest taking mental breaks along the way.

I've found my Raison D'être. My reason to get up! To keep going! To live! FIND YOURS! I'm here to inspire. I'm here to be an example of what breaking cycles looks like, and to shatter expectations. We all must die. When I'm gone grieve for me, but keep living and never be afraid to sprinkle a little Sugar in Your Grits.

Reference Page

1. Nietzsche, Friedrich (1889). Götzen-Dämmerung. Germany. Verlag von C. G. Naumann

2. Italian translated to English. Love at first sight

3. Simpson, Virginia. "Grief Quotes". https://www.drvirginiasimpson.com/grief-quotes-2/

4. Lewes, George Henry (1846). The Spanish Drama, Life of Lope De Vega.   W. Clowes and Sons, Stamford Street

5. Aeschylus. Agamemnon. Circa 525/524 BC

6. King, Martin Luther. 1959. The Measure of a Man. Christian Education Press

Hotline Information:

Domestic Violence Hotline 1-800-799-SAFE (7233)

www.thehotline.org

National Suicide Prevention Lifeline 1-800-273-8255

suicidepreventionlifeline.org

Contact Information

www.jdelanopublishing.com

email: info@jdelanopublishing.com

www.acallendergirl.com

email: amanda@acallendergirl.com

JDelano Publishing

P.O Box 522

Lincoln Park, New Jersey 07035

Social Media Information

Instagram: AmandaYCallender

Twitter: @acallendergirl

IN LOVING MEMORY OF

NADIYAH JEAN JOHNSON

JUNE 15, 1978 - DECEMBER 08, 2008